Godfrey

A SPECIAL TIME
REMEMBERED

Godfrey

A SPECIAL TIME
REMEMBERED

Jill Bennett
and Suzanne Goodwin

HODDER AND STOUGHTON
LONDON SYDNEY AUCKLAND TORONTO

British Library Cataloguing in Publication Data

Bennett, Jill, *19—*
    Godfrey.
    1. Tearle, Godfrey   2. Bennett, Jill
    I. Title   II. Goodwin, Suzanne
    729'.028'0922   PN2598.T/

    ISBN 0-340-33160-7

For Orme
The real thing

ILLUSTRATIONS

Godfrey Seymour Tearle[1]
Godfrey's father, Osmond Tearle[1]
Godfrey aged eight and a half[1]
His design for a bi-plane[1]
Godfrey as Silvius in *As You Like It*[2]
Godfrey with Cathleen Nesbitt in *Quality Street*[3]
A scene from *Quality Street*[3]
A scene from *The Amazons*[2]
An article Godfrey wrote on acting[1]
Another on women[1]
Theatre postcard[1]
His fan-mail photograph[1]
A scene from *The Land of Promise*[1]
With Madge Titheradge in *The Garden of Allah*[3]
A scene from *The Sign on the Door*[3]
The golfing actor[1]
Godfrey as Lieutenant-Colonel Waverley Ango in *The Faithful Heart*[3]
Scenes from *The Faithful Heart*[1]
A theatre poster[2]
From a page of Godfrey's 1923 notices[1]
Godfrey in the "comedy fantasy" *Arlequin*[2]
A theatre cartoon[4]
The programme for *The Acquittal*[1]
Godfrey with his wife, Mary Malone[3]
Godfrey as Hamlet[2]
The Boy David[1]
Godfrey and Margaret Rawlings in *The Flashing Stream*[3]
A still from *One of our Aircraft is Missing*[5]
Godfrey in Hitchcock's *The Thirty-Nine Steps*[6]

Illustrations

On holiday in Madeira[1]
A silver dressing-table set, a present from Godfrey[1]
My first good film role – *Hell Below Zero*[14]
Hell Below Zero[14]
Publicity shots[14]
A studio shot[14]
The last photo of Godfrey[1]
As Pamela in *Time Present*[15]
Pamela refusing to go to Orme's funeral[16]
Poster for *Time Present*[1]

ACKNOWLEDGMENTS

1   Personal collection
2   Illustrated London News Picture Library
3   The Mander and Mitchenson Theatre Collection
4   *Punch*
5   By courtesy of National Telefilm Associates
6   Still from the film *The Thirty-Nine Steps* by courtesy of The Rank
    Organisation PLC
7   Angus McBean photograph, Harvard Theatre Collection
8   By courtesy of Metro-Goldwyn-Mayer
9   Angus McBean
10 Camera Press
11 By courtesy of Vic Films Ltd.
12 By courtesy of EMI
13 By courtesy of Romulus Films
14 By courtesy of Columbia Pictures
15 John Timbers
16 The *Observer*

GODFREY SEYMOUR TEARLE was the son of a notable late Victorian actor, Osmond Tearle, and Marianne Conway, an American actress who belonged to a famous theatre family. Godfrey Tearle began playing in his father's company when he was eight years old. He later became what was called a matinee idol. His good looks and magnificent voice, his talent and an irresistible stage presence, made him into a star.

There are a few of his films sometimes still shown on television. Hitchcock's *Thirty-Nine Steps*, for instance, and his last, the Ealing comedy *The Titfield Thunderbolt*. But although Tearle made many films, beginning in the silent days, he did not rate himself as a film actor. It was the stage which he commanded, and theatre audiences loved him.

Like the arc of a rainbow, his career stretched across a huge panorama of the English theatre. As a child he met Henry Irving. He grew up in the days of great actor-managers of late Victorian and Edwardian style . . . Beerbohm Tree, George Alexander. He went through the Great War, acted during the hectic twenties in Shakespeare, in musicals, in farces; he played West End comedies which lightened the sombre thirties, went through another war . . . to arrive one cold spring day in 1949 at the Shakespeare Memorial Theatre at Stratford-on-Avon, where this story begins.

JILL BENNETT was born in Penang. Her father started a merchant firm and owned rubber plantations there and her parents lived in colonial style. Jill was their only child. When war broke out in the Far East her mother brought her back to England. Her father was taken prisoner by the Japanese, and neither Jill nor her mother saw him for the next five years.

There was no acting tradition in the Bennett family, but Jill showed an early talent for ballet and studied it at school. Then at fifteen she chose acting instead of dancing – she decided to go to drama school, the Royal Academy of Dramatic Art.

She was given one speaking part and walk-ons in the Shakespeare Memorial Theatre company's 1949 season. It was there that she first met Godfrey Tearle.

One

You are supposed eventually to get over love. Nobody
can pine for ever. It becomes a self-indulgent invention, like Queen Victoria keeping rooms full of Albert's
clothes, or Miss Havisham in *Great Expectations* stop-
ping the clocks and letting mice eat the wedding cake.
So what I am writing will look far-fetched and even
impossible. Yet it is the plain truth. I never *have* got
over the man I loved when I was very young. I have no
packets of letters; no albums of photographs. Possessions bored him; he had had too many in the past, and
when he died, leaving me the contents of his flat, I
gave away the most evocative things, so convinced
was I that since I had his love I needed nothing else.
That wasn't right but I didn't know it then. I didn't
know either that the four years we had spent together
were going to affect my life for bad as well as for good.
Much of what we shared was full of joy, but he still cast
his long shadow across my future, influenced the way
I look at people and the way I work. I'm sure he
guessed that and it bothered him. I didn't guess. I was
too busy living – happy, flattered, proud, and later
painfully anxious. A love affair is like riding a surf
board in twenty-foot waves. If you fall off you can
break your neck.

I met Godfrey Tearle when I was very young, a naïve
beginner full of nervous self-confidence. He was an
exceedingly famous actor, already a legend in the
theatre, more than forty years older than I, and light
years away from me in experience, fame and knowledge. It's a shock to realise how many people today
have never heard of him. It proves what we know, that

the theatre in its essence is as ephemeral as scent. Intensely powerful at the time and then gone for ever. The thorn that I've never managed and probably never wanted to dig out of myself is that after Godfrey died his effect on me did not. He looms heroic in my imagination. I am dazzled by him still. Yet in a way I resist calling what we shared a love affair; I prefer to call it a passionate friendship. But whatever love it is that I have for Godfrey, I never have got over him, and when I write that down and look at it I'm sure he would think it ridiculous.

My mother first took me to see him in 1947 when he was playing Antony to Edith Evans as Cleopatra. He had had a huge success and people called his performance one of genius – he *was* the great soldier, aged and softened and fallen by weakness to become Cleopatra's slave. My mother belonged to the Edwardian generation who had adored Godfrey Tearle as a great matinee idol. She had sat in theatres when, at the end of the play, the women in the audience pelted him with flowers as if he were a victorious Roman general. Godfrey played every kind of part, from the suave hero of drawing-room comedy to the priest torn between the lure of sex and the life of the soul. He never stopped acting, and women never stopped falling in love with him. Sometimes they literally threw diamonds and pearls at him. When he told me that I laughed. Did he dodge? Did he give the jewels to a hospital? Or to one of his wives? I don't remember hearing the answer, and the only treasure I have left from all that worship is an ebony God of Wisdom which a Russian princess threw at his feet. That certainly hasn't fulfilled its promise.

Seeing him play Antony, I was enthralled. I was also fascinated to see that good acting looked so easy. Yes, it did look easy and I was pretty sure that it was, although I had not thought so when I was at R.A.D.A.

There I had begun brilliantly, so I was told, and steadily grown worse and worse.

Actors, for all their much-vaunted humility, are arrogant and never more so than when they are young. The Stratford-on-Avon theatre was in the news that year. It had had brilliant seasons recently under Barry Jackson, the founder of the Birmingham Repertory Theatre, and now in 1949 Anthony Quayle was taking over as the new director. Quayle was a thirty-five-year-old actor who had also been one of Barry Jackson's team of directors, and he was greatly admired. Stratford was definitely the place to be. Yet I was not particularly surprised when, with no experience, I was asked to join the company. I was given an audition in London by Anthony Quayle and three other directors, John Gielgud, Michael Benthall and Tyrone Guthrie. By the time it came to my turn, the company had been fully cast. I suppose the auditions went on merely because they had been arranged, and directors are always interested to see new actors, even when there is no job for them. Knowing there wasn't any room left in the company, I still went to the audition. That's something I wouldn't dream of doing now. I had a kind of determination. And when you are young what have you to lose? Afterwards Anthony Quayle asked me to his pretty little house in Pelham Street, Chelsea. "I haven't room for you in the company," he said, "but I've decided to make room." He added that he would give me the role of Bianca in *Othello*, and walk-ons in the other five Stratford productions. I accepted with becoming gratitude.

But when I went home to my parents' flat in Westbourne Terrace, I looked up *Othello* and thought Bianca, "mistress to Cassio", a pretty unimpressive part. I counted her lines. Thirty-seven. It never occur-

15

length manner of royalty and we treated them with considerable deference. I was glad to be among people of my own age. Everybody seemed to be discussing Godfrey Tearle who had not yet arrived. Some of the actors had played with him in the previous season's *Othello* in which he had had an enormous success. Whether the actors had played with him or not they all declared that he was wonderful. I was very curious to see him.

There was a lull in the talk when, with Anthony Quayle beside him, Godfrey Tearle finally ambled in. He had the strangest walk. I've often thought that it was like a gorilla's; he had long arms and they swung, yet he had an extraordinary grace. Watching from a distance, I decided that my mother's idol looked nouveau riche. His clothes were stylish pale-coloured plus fours, he was tall and impressive, and the most noticeable thing about him was charm. Even then, charm was something rarely met in anybody under thirty. In older people it was beginning to be thin on the top. Not with Godfrey Tearle. Each of the actors was introduced, looking impressed and respectful, and he shook hands with a pleasant smile. He had the formality of Edwardian good manners, yet they rang true. I had never seen anybody so polite in my life.

The big names came first, most of whom he knew and warmly greeted. Then it was the turn of the supporting players.

"This is Margaret Courtenay . . ."

"This is Timothy Bateson . . ."

Since I had been given nothing to do in *Macbeth* but play an apparition which rises out of the witches' boiling cauldron in a dark cave in Act IV, I was not interested in all the boring introductions. I wasn't part of them and merely stood at the end of a row of actors and watched.

"And this," said Anthony Quayle, as a fine up-standing actor of about twenty-three, with a mop of wavy hair and a good profile, stepped forward, "is Eric Lander who will be playing Fleance."

Godfrey Tearle took Eric Lander's hand with the same friendly politeness. But he shook his head.

"Oh no. No, no, I'm afraid he won't do at all."

Silence.

Until now it had all been going swimmingly. Anthony Quayle and Eric Lander were extremely taken aback.

Godfrey Tearle was firm.

"I'm afraid he's much too big and much too good-looking. Fleance has to look like a child."

He began to pace slowly down the line of actors and actresses, studying each in turn. Everybody was quiet. At the very end of the line he came to me.

He stopped, took a step backwards and studied me with his head on one side. He said his courteous, "How do you do, Miss. . . ?"

"Jill Bennett," put in Anthony Quayle.

Pointing a long elegant hand towards me, Godfrey Tearle said, "She'll do for Fleance."

I didn't hear another word that anyone said. I was sunk in shame. Was this why I had come to Stratford? To play *a child – and male?* The meeting ended and the actors trailed out. I had nobody to complain to, there wasn't even an eye to catch. I certainly wasn't going to telephone my parents and wail to them. If I'm going to be humiliated, I thought, that's my problem. I walked gloomily back to my digs and gave my sweet ration to my landlady. She was deeply grateful.

The thing about first rehearsals if you have a small part, particularly one you never wanted, is that you can't feel that what is going on is important. Some directors don't make supporting players wait about – Anthony Quayle didn't – and when the leading

19

actors rehearse their big scenes, the other actors are not called.

I felt bored when that happened, but didn't enjoy it when I *was* called. Both my scenes were with Banquo, played by Leon Quartermaine who had a sardonic Mephistophelean face and was quite elderly. I thought he didn't look strong. I worried about him in the scene where he had to fight the three murderers, all of whom were hearty muscular actors in their twenties. Perhaps my anxiety for Leon was because of my father's health, which had never been good since he came home from being a prisoner of war. Perhaps Leon really was frail. He certainly wasn't when we played our scenes, and before the second one he and I had to hurry under the stage to make our entrance. He used to charge ahead of me in the dark, hissing, "Come *on*, Boy!"

My costume fittings for Fleance were a nightmare. The first time I put on the costume I took one look at myself in the long glass in the Wardrobe, and went into a deep sulk. I had to wear a lot of leather which was to make me look tough, and furry coverings over my fat girl's knees, and lots of brown body make-up which we call bole. All the men had to be brown, the director said, because they lived out of doors in the wild Scottish rain and wind. They must look weatherbeaten. As I was one of the chaps and was being brought up to fight, I must be weatherbeaten too. Lady Macbeth and Lady Macduff, I noticed enviously, were to be white as lilies.

After Banquo had been murdered and Fleance had escaped, I got ready for my next appearance as the phantom who rises out of the cauldron and tells Macbeth to be "bloody, bold, and resolute". Shakespeare describes the apparition as that of a bloody child. Every time I sat in the bath moodily washing off the bole before reaching for the blood I used to think, "This is not what I expected."

At the first dress rehearsal before the beginning of the "double, double, toil and trouble" scene, I was wearing my apparition costume and well smeared with blood when I took my place to wait behind the witches' cauldron. The witches, all played by men, had not yet begun to chant, but there were loud rolling peals of thunder. A man came and sat quietly down beside me. Looking round, I saw that it was Godfrey Tearle.

Love never seems to give an advance warning. If it did, most of us would run. I had no idea when that big celebrated man sat down on the bench next to me that he and I would ever become friends. We simply happened to be waiting in the same place.

The sets and costumes for *Macbeth*, by Edward Carrick, were very barbaric, with great rough stone slabs, monoliths, shaggy costumes. The cauldron was at the top of what looked like a dark mountain. When the apparitions were summoned forth, they went upwards and appeared in clouds of billowing smoke. Macbeth came downwards towards the witches. So Godfrey and I sat waiting for our entrances which were within a few lines of each other.

I've said that leading actors used to behave in the cool and distant manner of royalty. He never did. I had an idea that he really liked me. I also thought he was feeling guilty because he had singled me out for Fleance, and it was his fault that I felt daunted. But he was very funny to talk to, and I'm quite witty sometimes. We sat behind the dark mountain and made each other laugh.

It must have been obvious that I detested Fleance's costume. I had been lamenting about it loudly to people. One day when I was at a costume fitting, Godfrey wandered in as if by accident. He studied me for a while and finally said,

"Good. Good. You wouldn't know she's a girl."

Of course as an actor I wanted to look like a boy. But I was a girl and I wanted to look like one as well. I was sulkier than ever after he said that.

I had to brace myself for a lot of things. For the fittings. For dress parades. For being looked at in an unnerving way. This happens in an actor's life from the beginning and I have always hated it. You have to peel off your clothes while the designer and director are there. You have to stand about in your under-clothes. There is a particular horror about being stu-died as if you are a piece of furniture to be used by them. They speak about you as if you aren't yourself but an object – their object.

"If she had her hair done so . . ."

"If she wore . . ."

I didn't tell Godfrey how I felt about that, but he seemed to know. After the Wardrobe visit he sud-denly said,

"You must remember that you could be king of Scotland."

He was silent for a moment and then he said reflect-ively,

"Small parts are always terrible. You haven't time to fail. You have to come on and be wonderful at once."

The next time we rehearsed the scene where Mac-beth meets Banquo and Fleance inside the castle, Godfrey stood with his back to the stage, facing me. He told me to stand centre stage. Then he said,

"Defy me. Stare me out. Go on, stare me out. And remember that you could be king of Scotland."

I had a feeling of power every time I did that.

We became friendly during the long days of rehear-sals. I was fascinated to watch him work. I've read theatre critics who said that Godfrey was inherently lazy and liked to take things easily, but that was not true. He did work – very hard. But he was mysterious because he was a star.

We had got into the habit of sitting together back-stage and behind the cauldron. I didn't think how I felt about that, I just looked forward to our little chats. Then one day he asked me to lunch with him the following Sunday. Of course I said yes, and spent a good deal of time after that wondering what I ought to wear, what on earth we would talk about, and how soon he would find out that I was pig ignorant. But I need not have bothered, because the next time we were waiting for our entrances he cancelled the date. He was so very sorry, he said with that annoying charm, but a friend had telephoned and was coming from London.

Having a second bath – there was one for washing off the bole and another for washing off the blood – I realised that I was very upset. I had been dreading the lunch. Now it was off, my disappointment shocked me.

On Sunday morning I decided to go to the Dirty Duck with some friends in the company to cheer myself up. The Dirty Duck was the actors' name for an old rambling pub near the theatre, called the Black Swan. It is built up some steps which overlook the gardens and the river. During the season it was and still is packed with actors and buzzing with talk. When I arrived that sunny morning, the first person I saw was Godfrey. He was leaning against the door, a tall negligent sort of Gary Cooper, dry martini in hand. Heaven knows how he managed to get a martini at the Duck. The woman with him had a cloud of grey hair, wore wildly expensive-looking tweeds in Lovat blue, and ankle socks. She was attractive and extremely old, all of thirty-five. Catching my eye, Godfrey winked. I looked dignified and respectful, went to the far end of the bar, and then got rather drunk on cider.

He did take me out to lunch after all on the following

Sunday. We drove to Malvern in his car; it was an open Triumph Dolomite, bright emerald with red leather inside. Godfrey enjoyed owning a rakish car; it was the first two-seater he'd ever had. In his matinee idol past it had been a Rolls or a Daimler with a uniformed chauffeur.

It was bright and cold and we drove with the hood down. The early April country was green, everything was springing and budding, there were lambs in the fields, and at the edge of the road were thick clumps of celandines. Godfrey drove well and was in marvellous spirits. That did me good, for I was feeling daunted again. I had decided that my fantasies when I'd arrived in Stratford looked pretty pathetic. I was not going to be the English Katharine Hepburn. I was not even going to be discovered as Jill Bennett. During lunch I ate a great deal to cheer myself up.

Robert Morley was in the hotel restaurant surrounded by his family. There was his son Sheridan, who was at prep school nearby, and whom they had come to see, and Robert Morley's father-in-law, Captain Herbert Buckmaster, who had been married to Gladys Cooper. He owned Buck's Club in Clifford Street and was the inventor of the now-famous drink Buck's Fizz, a delicious mixture of champagne and orange juice. Godfrey introduced me to everybody. He was not at all flummoxed to be seen out with Fleance; on the contrary he seemed delighted about it. The cliché that youth was on my side turned out not to be true. I found that I was the one who had to be on my mettle . . .

On some mornings when I walked from my digs to the theatre, I saw a familiar broad-shouldered figure pacing the Bancroft lawns. It was Godfrey going through his lines. He was always alone and completely absorbed, walking with that graceful swing and staring at the grass. No one came up and spoke to him. If the townspeople going by recognised him, and they must have done, they left him alone. Stars used to have that kind of freedom.

The sun shone all day before the opening of *Macbeth*; although it was only April, the weather was wonderful. Stratford, so quiet and empty when we actors had arrived, was suddenly packed with visitors. People sunbathed on the lawns outside the theatre, and took boats out on the river. The cherry and almond trees were in flower. In the evening, the theatre was floodlit for the first time since the war, and the trees along the edge of the river were threaded with coloured lights which reflected in the water. It was all exciting and festive, and the crowds began to pour towards the theatre.

It was a night of enormous importance for Godfrey, the fulfilment of an ambition which had been with him all during his acting life. He saw Macbeth as the most challenging part among Shakespeare's great tragic figures. Critics and audiences always thought of Godfrey as a leading actor who played heroes. He was tall and commanding, he had a voice which he used with wonderful skill and he could make audiences weep. He had both power and physical beauty, but people had a fixed idea about him. One critic nicknamed him after the worthy, unadventurous and reliable character in Thackeray's *Vanity Fair*: "the Dobbin of the English stage". Godfrey disliked that. He disliked, too, the reputation he had for being the theatre's Mister Nice. He wasn't nice – nobody is if he is any good.

Though he had always longed to play Macbeth he knew that the part was fiendishly difficult, for Macbeth is the only one of Shakespeare's tragic heroes who is damned, and the play, alone among the great tragedies, is wholly concerned with evil. Hazlitt said that we could conceive of nobody to play the part properly, nobody to look like a man who had met the Weird Sisters. Few actors had disproved that, and certainly none in Godfrey's time. He had seen many fail. Macbeth haunted him, and now at last here was his chance.

There are a strange number of disasters linked to the play's history. Actors so believe in the play's ill luck that they will not quote stray lines in their dressing-rooms, and most of them refuse even to name *Macbeth*; they call it The Scottish Play. Once the actor in the title role was accidentally wounded in the last fight and later he died of his wounds. In the nineteenth century, during performances of *Macbeth* at Covent Garden there were riots, and in New York the military were called out and twenty people were killed. In the 1920s at the Royal Court Theatre the dress circle caught fire and the scenery collapsed, and at the Old Vic during performances of *Macbeth* there was a run of accidents and injuries. We never imagined that our first night was destined to join that ominous list of disasters. But at the beginning of Lady Macbeth's sleepwalking scene, Diana Wynyard overbalanced and fell from the top of an unbalustraded staircase down to the stage below, almost breaking her ankle. She went on playing in great pain.

But before that, Godfrey had met his own misfortune. When we were sitting in our familiar place behind the cauldron he said to me in a low voice.

"I'm not getting it right."

I didn't know what to answer. On the previous night at the last dress rehearsal he had been breathtaking; and didn't he have a great safety net of talent and experience?

"I could be better. So much better," he said.

I was nervous and harassed and sat beside him, saying nothing.

Fordham Flower, who was the theatre's chairman

and whose family had built the theatre, gave a lavish party after the performance, and we were all invited. There was the usual excited talk by actors keyed up after a first night. There was champagne. I saw Godfrey in the distance, surrounded by friends who had driven from London to see the play. He had changed into a dinner jacket and looked handsome and self-possessed – a star. I kept remembering the actor in his rough Chieftan's costume sitting beside me. I wished I could talk to him, but it was impossible now.

Parties like this always go on for a long time. There's an after-the-first-night feeling and the actors simply stand or sit and go on talking until dawn. I supposed it was going to be like that. A few people began to dance in a desultory way, and I was watching them when Godfrey, who had stayed long enough for good manners, suddenly walked across the room and spoke to me.

"I'll drive you home."

It was extraordinary of him to say that in front of everyone – in this company where people were called Mister and Miss. The theatre was very bourgeois and snobbish and inelastic and he cut through all that. What he did seems a small thing now, but it wasn't then. I didn't answer, I just walked out of the room beside him.

We got into his car and he drove through the silent town.

"Do you mind if we go for a drive?" he said.

He drove for what seemed a long time down empty country roads, and when he stopped at last we were by a great desolate place of flat treeless fields. It was a disused airfield.

"Shall we get out and walk?"

He opened the car door for me and we went across into a huge emptiness of rough grass stretching into

27

nowhere. I suppose it must have been flooded by moonlight after that bright day but I don't remember anything romantic like that. I only remember that we walked, and how he talked to me, saying that he had failed. The timing of a performance was vital, he said, it had to be right, it had to be perfectly right. Everything had gone as it should on the previous evening, he had been on his mettle, had been perfectly equipped, and the flair which was essential for him had been there. He needed that, because technique was easy for him. It was the flair, the fire, which made him dangerous. But he had used it all up last night, there had been one rehearsal too many. At tonight's performance he had been tired in the wrong way. He was so dreadfully disappointed. He kept saying that it was a failure, a real failure, as we walked in that deserted rather awful place. He walked with long strides, that gorilla-like walk which was so much part of him, both shambling and graceful, and I had to hurry to keep up.

It was the first time in my life that I had heard a real actor, a famous actor at the top of his profession, talk about his performance straight from the heart. He was doubting himself aloud. He spoke without a trace of self-indulgence, I don't think he'd had more than one glass of wine. He was just himself, truthful and desperately disappointed.

I had never been confided in like that before, never had my opinion asked or been taken seriously. It wasn't possible, as it had not been when we sat together during the play, to say that I thought he had been marvellous. That wasn't part of the deal. I scarcely spoke. I was dumbfounded. We were just two actors, one who couldn't do anything yet and one who was a bloody genius. I think I loved him very much that night.

It was such an astounding thing for him to do, such a huge generous gesture, such a risk. I remember I began to feel very cold and Godfrey took off his jacket and made me wear it.

Then he drove me home. He shook my hand and said "Thank you".

It was unlike anything people must have thought when we drove away earlier in that flashy car, unlike everything it seemed to be. It was as if we had made a promise, he and I: a contract of honour.

Two

Sometimes when you first wake up there is a moment when you don't remember yesterday. You're still free of it. It is horrible when what comes rushing towards you a moment later is the remembrance of grief. And an undeserved delight when you had forgotten happiness. The morning after the *Macbeth* opening I didn't have that moment of forgetting. I remembered what had happened, but with a feeling of sheer disbelief. It was as if I had made the whole thing up. But although the time I had spent last night walking with Godfrey Tearle seemed unreal, I still dreaded the notices. I hoped that he had been wrong.

That is the odd thing about being an actor. You don't *know* you have had a success or a failure. I've played at first nights when the audiences cheered, and the notices the next day have been bad. I have faced a cold house and woken, incapable of forgetting *that*, to discover I am in a success. Notices always matter. One pretends that they don't. But they do.

It was Sunday and I had a sense of complete anti-climax. I'm given to those and I don't cope with them well, just as I am not good at ordinary life. I was in a bored restless mood when I went out into the April sun to buy the newspapers. I didn't look at them at once, but walked across the Bancroft lawns in front of the theatre and sat on the river wall. Then I read the notices. They were good. More than good. Ivor Brown in the *Observer* wrote that "Godfrey Tearle has one by one assailed the great Shakespearean roles. He does it rather later in life than usual for such an undertaking . . . but with the benefit of great experience and with

30

the physical equipment of one who is just as young as he feels. The Macbeth which he showed us tonight is a magnificent addition to his portrait gallery." He managed, went on Ivor Brown, to speak like a poet, behave like a soldier – and a murderer. It was a triumph. Harold Hobson in *The Sunday Times* called him "the powerful soldier, wild and shaggy, embarrassed by compliments", and although there was no suggestion of "the tormented poet, whose imagination is touched off by a hairspring of horror" until the dagger scene, then his appearance was electrifying and there was a world of agony in the words "dagger of the mind". In the quieter passages "there is a beautiful and silver melancholy".

It felt strange to be sitting in the sun and reading the notices of a famous actor, knowing how *he* felt about his own performance. In those days the critics had a true perspective of the theatre. Ivor Brown, Harold Hobson, A. V. Cookman, W. A. Darlington, J. C. Trewin, Philip Hope-Wallace and T. C. Worsley – all were perceptive, imaginative and penetrating. I have an idea that critics now are more aware of the demands of their readers; that they're more journalists than critics.

I was relieved when I read the excellent notices and for a moment I relaxed. But then I remembered. The Sunday critics had come to the dress rehearsal. And that had been the performance which Godfrey knew had gone right.

What did Godfrey do on that Sunday? I never even asked him. It didn't once cross my mind during the long day to telephone him, which might have been a friendly thing to do. To go round and see him with a bunch of flowers would have been a gesture. I made none. I left it all to him.

In spite of the sunshine and the cheerful river the day crawled, for what is slower than a provincial

Sunday? I was really glad that I had to be in the theatre early the next morning for a rehearsal of *Much Ado About Nothing*. It is true that I had been given nothing to do in the play, except to saunter across the stage carrying a bunch of prop lilies; but at least I didn't have to face another dragging day by myself. I was also understudying the role of Margaret and I didn't like that much – Margaret was a gentlewoman. I just learned the lines and the moves as quickly as I could and thought no more about it.

During the lunch break I went out and bought four daily newspapers. This time when I read them I felt sick. The notices were exactly what Godfrey had expected.

The Times began, "Alas, the first modern actor to bring the heaven-defying Macbeth of literature to the stage has still to appear. Hopes that he might be Godfrey Tearle . . . came to surprisingly little last [Saturday] night: to be the best Othello of the time is perhaps enough for glory." The *Daily Mail* said kindly that it should become magnificent when he got into his stride, but that last night something had been missing. And the *Daily Telegraph* quoted Hazlitt's belief that Macbeth as a part was impossible to act, and added that Godfrey Tearle's performance had left the critic unsatisfied.

The rehearsals for *Much Ado* went on all day. I kept thinking about Godfrey. I know now that a lot of actors really do not read their notices, or put off reading them for a week – even a month – after the opening. Praise or blame can both have a disturbing effect on a performance. But I was new in this tightrope world, and I imagined Godfrey reading every single word and being hurt by it. His intelligence would agree with the critics; he would know that his performance had been found out. Yet the fact that they wrote exactly what he'd said to me on the airfield was not the point.

Because they were right did not make his disappointment less.

When the rehearsal finally ended, I walked out of
the rehearsal room and under the arch which joins
what is left of the old theatre, burned down in the
twenties, to the modern building. Suddenly I saw
Godfrey. He was leaning elegantly by the stage door
and rolling a cigarette with one hand. It was a trick of
his which I later learned he had used to great effect in
drawing-room comedies.

Seeing me, he grinned. And I thought with a rush of
total pleasure – I didn't make the whole thing up.

An actor's life can be wonderful or disastrous, funny
or frustrating. What you need all the time as much as
your talent is stamina. There isn't an actor who does
not dread going out on to a stage to play on the
evening after bad notices. We feel certain that everybody in the theatre has read them. We have seen it in
the faces of fellow actors, a sort of pity. The moment
we come on, we feel it coming from the audience, a
sort of deadening. Later, meeting our friends, we
know they will be pleased. A lot of people are simply
delighted when you fail.

Godfrey went out on to that enormous Stratford stage and gave a wonderful performance that
night. There was not a sign of what he felt or what
they had written. His performance was strong and
passionate, and when he came to sit beside me in the
dark, he was relaxed. He could survive success and
failure.

I've always been a slow burner in love and in
friendship. I am amused and disbelieving, perhaps I
envy the idea of that thing they call love at first sight.
Being quite blind and seeing most things in a blur, how
could I recognise it in any case? Does it exist? I suppose

it must do. Dante only looked at Beatrice when she was eight years old, yet later wrote "my soul that in her looks Found all contentment". It never has been like that for me. Except with Godfrey.

After the night when he chose me to be with him at a time of bitter disappointment we never went back on what we had tacitly promised. We never *said* anything, but neither of us doubted that there was a bond. On the first morning I had woken up and could not believe it had happened at all, but that feeling soon wore off. After a few days I was taking Godfrey's affection for me, and mine for him, for granted. I accepted them. It is only as you get older that you become fearful. Everything is too complicated, too thought-about. It is easy to read all kinds of heavy mistaken meanings into a look or a gesture. I was very young and very open, and I accepted Godfrey's company with ease. I think he was probably a slow burner in love as well. Certainly for a famous worldly man he was reserved and shy. I only realised much later that he already knew time was not on his side.

We began to meet every day. We used to have morning coffee in a Tudor teashop in Sheep Street. It is still there and I daresay as popular as ever – it's called the Cobweb. We sat at a table in the corner, and I ate homemade cakes and Godfrey didn't. There was always a lot to talk about. He liked chat, both talking and listening, he was a great listener and it was easy to make him laugh. John Dexter came to Stratford once and saw us together in the Cobweb. He said years later "You both looked wonderful together. But I remember thinking – how very extraordinary."

Godfrey *was* wonderful to be with. His personality was relaxed, yet he always seemed larger than life. The strongest impression was of his astonishing voice which he used like a musical instrument. It had become second nature to him to do that.

I was very busy enjoying myself, running down the street to the Cobweb or jumping into Godfrey's car. If the Stratford theatre and its company were rather like school and pupils, as a junior junior, being given too much attention by the head prefect, I was causing raised eyebrows. But I had no idea Godfrey and I were being noticed and talked about.

I have not mentioned our exact ages, and I don't want to. Journalists like to put labels on people, "Starlet, 20", "Balding, 50", "Miss World, 34-21-34". I suppose they find it a useful shorthand. But giving Godfrey's age and mine when we first became friends doesn't describe the way we were: it seems to falsify it. He was younger than my friends and I were in many ways. And I was busy trying to look and be much older – thirty-five at least. I felt that to be too young was letting him down. So there was a mixture of time. Godfrey had fame and knowledge and a sense of fun. I was very childish, but comfortable with older people. We both knew how to span the years that could have separated us.

At that time, Godfrey was staying at the Arden hotel, just across the road from the theatre. I haven't been to Stratford lately, and not into the Arden for years, and I am sure it is much changed. In those days it was like a high-class seaside guest house run by ladies out of *Cranford*. It was spotlessly clean and genteel. The oak tables in the dining room were polished like glass and placed too near each other. Little mats were scattered about, and amateurish water colours of Warwickshire hung on the walls. There were vases of garden flowers. I don't remember a bar, and the *Cranford* ladies were fussed when you asked for a drink. Perhaps they had only just acquired a licence.

During the early weeks of our friendship, Godfrey casually told me that he had decided to leave the

Arden. He was going, he said, to move to the Welcombe, the large stylish hotel in its own grounds, on a hill slightly outside the town. The homespun atmosphere of the Arden had never really suited the taste of a man who liked the splendour of what he called gin palaces. Besides, he thought the Arden was much too near the theatre, literally a step across the road to the stage door. Suddenly Godfrey found that he was having a very good time, as I was. He was racing about the countryside in his open car, and sharing the fun of the season with a new, if naïve friend. The Arden didn't exactly suit what he had in mind for himself and me.

There is a point between a man and a woman when either you jump into the deep water or you stay permanently in the shallows. The moment of decision does not only happen in love, it happens in hate as well. I've sometimes thought it is very like standing at the top of a precipitate hill. You have time to draw back into safety. Or you can deliberately begin to move, slowly at first, then faster and faster down the steep hill until at last you are thrown into the sea.

I don't know if I fell in love with Godfrey. I question the words in love when I think about him and me. There's such a lot of ego about being in love, it is a very selfish act. I just loved and I had everything I wanted. Of course the space of years, a great map of time, lay between us. Godfrey noticed that to my detriment. My total lack of knowledge was often the despair of both of us.

We were careful with each other during those first weeks. We were happy and affectionate but we both knew that this was not a flirtation, and that to be fond of each other was very dangerous. So dangerous that as the days went by we saw that it was going to be simple. We didn't play games at each other's expense, and I never had a moment of thinking that I would give him up. We knew instinctively that neither of us was going to fail or betray the other.

I am sure he thought a lot about whether to have a love affair with me. I know I would have accepted it if all we had been was close friends. But because he was a beautiful man, it was the natural development for us. I think we both welcomed it with delight and pleasure and amazement. Both of us were puritans, in a way.

The irony for Godfrey was that I was the last thing he had expected or wanted to happen to him. He had never wished to be tied to anybody again; he had been tied for most of his life. He had always had a wife since he'd been very young (he was married three times). His last marriage to Barbara Mary Palmer had ended in divorce a few years before, and now, at the height of his fame, what Godfrey wanted was some fun. He was his own master now. He was flying solo. He never meant to become serious over me when we sat together behind the witches' cauldron, I was just one of a number of young actresses in the company. He was charming and friendly to everyone. But after the night on the airfield he found he could really talk to me. It sounds unlikely, but he had never, ever, had that before.

In love, we took each other by surprise. *He* knew at once that he was going to have a great effect on me and it gave him a sense of responsibility. I didn't know that and was just happy.

Our mutual life changed after he moved to the Welcombe. The hotel was very grand, with lofty rooms and a fine staircase. Godfrey had a garden suite, a large bedroom, bathroom and private sitting room with French windows opening on to the garden. He was naturally one for splendour; he'd lived on a grand scale for a long time and it suited him. Yet he was as adaptable as a chameleon. He was a true actor, a vagabond who took the richest places for granted yet was at home in shabby lodgings. He liked luxury. He never needed it.

There were six plays in the Stratford season and they seemed to follow each other fast, one on the heels of the next. I was playing every night, rehearsing all day and sometimes doing understudy rehearsals as well. I hated those, being convinced that no actress whom I understudied would be sporting enough to fall ill and allow me a chance. Paradoxically, I also felt that if she did I would not be good enough to take over. In any case, more paradox, the parts I was understudying were boring and meagre. They were all servants. Later in my career, Laurence Olivier told me that I was very bad at playing servants unless, he said, they had particularly complex characters . . .

The days were filled with dull work. The rehearsal room jangled to the sound of a tinny piano. We danced. We walked gracefully. We froze into studied groups. While our betters were playing the real scenes, we sat about not listening intelligently and learning, but bored out of our minds. Then at night the crowds came pouring towards the theatre; often they were of noticeable smartness and had come from London.

In spite of having so much work to do, we all managed to fit in a lot of fun. By the time the season was in full swing I had made some casual friends in the company. I used to make friends easily, although they were only work mates and the friendships did not go deep.

When Godfrey asked me to lunch with him at the Welcombe, he often invited a number of my friends too. Afterwards we played tennis. As I was to learn Godfrey was a generous host, he loved to give. He resembled the character in one of Henry James's books who "liked to invite people and to pay for them, and disliked to be invited and paid for". Godfrey was a giver – he was a dreadful taker, he hadn't the trick of it. Nobody was more difficult to give things to than Godfrey.

The Welcombe lunches were very popular with the actors and everybody wanted to be asked. One of the young actors who often came to lunch was Robert Shaw. He was in embryo what he became later, a stiff, aggressive, handsome, rasping kind of man, determined to assert his personality and make an impression. He was attractive, with short springy curling hair and unwavering blue eyes, and he had the oddest smile as if he were in pain. Physically tough, he was obsessed with fitness even then. I remember how cross he was when I beat him at tennis: he played to win. For a young man who had such a dashing personality, it was a surprise to us all when he failed his driving test because he had driven too slowly.

One hot summer afternoon he invited me out punting on the river. It was a favourite Sunday pastime for most of the younger members of the company during that hot summer, and Robert punted well. When we tied up in a quiet river backwater he made a sudden lunge at me. I gave him an indignant push and he landed in the river. Women, I thought, should be allowed to choose. Climbing back, spluttering, into the punt he was really furious. It was agony not to laugh as, still dripping, he punted me home.

Godfrey liked Robert Shaw but said to me once that he did not think he would succeed. "The trouble," Godfrey said, "is that his idea of acting is to face front and shout." Godfrey was wrong. Robert Shaw became a big star and a very rich man doing exactly what Godfrey described, facing front and shouting. Yet in some miraculous way he was a very, very good film actor.

All my friends seemed to be learning to drive just then. Godfrey said that he would teach me. "Every woman," he said, "should be able to drive. And should have her own money." It was rather like Virginia Woolf's dictum that every woman should have five hundred a year and a room of her own.

It was during my driving lessons that Godfrey and I had our first rows. Quite fierce ones, for if I was a clumsy pupil, Godfrey was no teacher. Later, in London, after I had twice crashed his beautiful car, he paid for me to be taught.

Taking the wheel firmly from me, Godfrey drove us out to lunch or supper, choosing the biggest and poshest country hotels. Many of these were the kind of hotels, like the Carlton in Cannes, where there are small lit alcoves in the hall and corridors, displaying large bottles of outrageously expensive scent. Godfrey stopped at one of these and bought me an outsized bottle of Lanvin's *My Sin*.

What, he said, could be more unsuitable?

We always went on expeditions which had a purpose. Sometimes it was to go to a particular hotel for a meal, or perhaps to look at a castle or a river view. As we drove through the country lanes we sang. One of Godfrey's favourites, which he taught me, was:

> Hello, my honey,
> Hello, my bunny,
> Hello, my ragtime girl.

An enormous success in New York, there was talk of bringing it to London (it didn't actually arrive at Drury Lane until 1951, two years later). Godfrey told me he had been asked if he would play the male lead, the older man with whom Nellie Forbush, played by Mary Martin, falls in love. "But," Godfrey was told, "you would have to take singing lessons for six months." Godfrey replied arrogantly that a month would be ample, and turned down the role. One of the songs now in his repertoire was "Some Enchanted Evening", rendered with spirit. I sang girls' songs. French ones had become the fashion and I sang, "Dîtes-moi pourquoi la vie est belle . . ."

When we were not singing we used to listen to his car radio – a pretty unusual thing to have in those days. I loved it. Once there was a play in which Godfrey was the lead. He listened, as absorbed as I was, and when it was finished and I said how good he had been, answered in a rather grand but larky way, "Ah. We can still show them a thing or two."

I hadn't nearly enough clothes for going about with a famous man whose suits were made by Hawes and Curtis, and whose fine cotton shirts came from Turnbull and Asser. I used to look in the wardrobe in the corner of my room at my digs and sigh "what *on earth* can I wear next?" Either I was going to look my best or I wouldn't go out at all. My mother, who seemed to know intuitively that I was in dire need, began to buy me some clothes. I did notice, too, that Godfrey had started to buy himself a quite inordinate amount of new clothes. His wardrobe changed and changed; he never seemed to wear the same thing twice. His figure was marvellous, and he told me with satisfaction that he could still wear the Sam Browne belt he had worn in the 1914–18 war. Stylish, handsome and unbelievably elegant, he never wore jewellery. An old gold watch given him by Owen Nares, a theatre star of the twenties and thirties, and a great friend. Cuff links. Dress studs. That was all.

With the weather still blazingly hot, we actors spent our lunchtime breaks from rehearsal in the gardens behind the picture gallery. That part of the theatre is all that has remained of the Victorian-Tudor building which to Bernard Shaw's delight was burned down in 1926. It was covered with ivy and looked very gothic. With the romantic building behind us, we sat on the grass getting sunburned. We were glad to be in the sun because all our work was in the dark.

I was earning twelve pounds a week that season. Godfrey told me that I should meet his accountant. I was very taken with the idea of having an accountant, particularly Godfrey's. Vallance Lodge looked after all the leading actors and film people at that time – he was a star in his job as his clients were in theirs. When he drove from London to see Godfrey, I was introduced to him in the theatre car park.

"This," said Godfrey to me, "is the man who understands that you can have a wonderful year earning nothing, and a rotten year earning a great deal of money."

I liked Vallance Lodge very much. He was kind and good looking, brilliant at his job, and his firm has looked after me ever since. Yet he had an unsophisticated side, he was an amateur actor who loved the theatre more as a fan than as an expert. The idea of wonderful years or a great deal of money both sounded very unlikely as I left Godfrey and his friend, and went off to another understudy rehearsal.

Godfrey had numbers of visitors who drove to Stratford from London to see the plays and dine with him. I wasn't always invited to join them at these dinners, and when I *was* asked I had to peer hopelessly again into my wardrobe. I met Brian Aherne who came to see Godfrey. People said he was the American's idea of the charming Englishman, and he was mine too. Charlton Heston also came to dine with us. He hadn't yet gone to Hollywood to become the epic hero. He had played Dolabella in Godfrey's *Antony and Cleopatra* in New York, and Godfrey got on with him well. He was young and very tall, and as rangy as a cowboy.

One Sunday Godfrey decided to take me on an expedition to Broadway in the Cotswolds. We would, he said, dine at the Lygon Arms. When we arrived at

the beautiful seventeenth-century hotel, the first person Godfrey saw as we came into the dining room was
the film director Michael Powell. There were en-
thusiastic greetings. I thought Powell looked rather
wicked, a monster with wonderfully bright blue eyes.
He and Godfrey had worked together during the war
on the film *One of Our Aircraft is Missing*. I remember
Godfrey told me afterwards how Michael had yelled at
him during a take. Godfrey used his eyes a lot, as an
actor does who has played most of his life in the
theatre. Sometimes he threw them upwards, sometimes made them swim. Michael Powell did not want
any of that and shouted, "Don't *Tearle* your eyes! *Turn*
them!"

Powell was planning his next movie, *Gone to Earth*,
and the leading lady of the film was with him that
evening. It was Jennifer Jones. I was interested to meet
her. She was a star, and was married then to David
Selznick, who produced *Gone With the Wind*. I thought
her serious and very intense, particularly when she
declared to Godfrey that to be playing at Stratford-on-
Avon must be the most marvellous thing in the world.
Why, she'd do anything to play there, even as a
walk-on. I bit back the desire to offer her Fleance . . .

But my work wasn't as disappointing as it had been
at the start of the season. I still resented playing
Banquo's son, and I had nothing in *Much Ado*, John
Gielgud's soon-to-be-legendary production, except to
wear an exquisite green and white dress (the production was designed by Mariano Andreu in high Renais-
sance style), and stand about while Diana Wynyard
and Anthony Quayle spiritedly quarrelled. We had,
however, begun to rehearse *A Midsummer Night's
Dream*. I was to play one of Titania's fairies.

The director was Michael Benthall. Kenneth Tynan
described him as "sleek, urbane, well-washed and
ruthless". Certainly he was handsome and had the

sort of conventional features which used to be popular
for romantic heroes in silent films. His voice was soft
and there was something about him which was not
unlike Terence Rattigan – both men seemed privi-
leged.

As a director, Michael had a flair for movement and
colour. He had directed many ballets and he delighted
in wonderful decor. It was Michael's influence which
affected the Stratford productions at that time, all of
which were breathtaking to look at. *The Dream*, designed by James Bailey, had a Victorian feeling about
it, not because there were any crinolines, but because
the sets and costumes looked like classical paintings
by Victorian artists. Theseus's palace really *was* in
Athens, with tall Corinthian pillars and crimson and
gold hangings. Then suddenly the scene changed to a
forest drenched in moonlight. The switch from one
world to the other was as brusque and magical as if it
had been done by Puck himself. As immortals, our
costumes were dark blue and green and glittering, and
the girls were practically bare-breasted. I was quite
shocked. Michael used the Mendelssohn score played
very loudly – music which audiences always love and
I have never been able to stand.

Working for Michael Benthall was interesting for me
because he gave me chances. The way an actor feels
about a director is ambivalent. It can be irritable and
dissatisfied, it is always dependent. We need the
director and rely on him; he is our fellow conspirator.
He encourages us to make fools of ourselves. What he
does not encourage is the actor's fatal desire to please
– I had that and it is something a lot of actors learn to
throw out of the window. Working for a good director
is one of the greatest things in the world. He makes
you feel confident, and you know you are a part of the
work and not a pawn. He helps you to take risks and to
stretch your imagination. The back of my head aches

when I've been working hard with a director. Is it, I've often asked myself, that I have been made to use the muscles of my brain?

Usually once the play is on we forget the director, and he forgets us. Except if we're lucky enough to work for one who is really great. Then he doesn't leave us. He comes to see us all the time, and gives us notes – which we long for. He is still on our side.

Michael Benthall liked me, and for the first time that season I felt I was being used. I'd trained as a dancer and had a feeling for music and movement. That pleased him. I also amused him and he nicknamed me Fairy Fraught and Fairy's-lost-her-head after I had made an unforgettable entrance during a rehearsal, arriving onstage facing the wrong way on the re-volve – backwards, in fact.

"Come along, Fairy Fraught," called Michael. "Show your paces."

A troupe from a Midland dancing school had been brought in for this production. Hot on nicknames, Michael called them The Birmingham Fairies. We be-haved badly to those poor serious-minded dancers, larking about and giggling while they went through their numbers. We were feeling superior. We were real actors, even if we were only playing fairies too. Or, in Robert Shaw's case in balletic make-up and green jerkin, a butch kind of gnome. Robert Hardy played a gnome too but he was a cleverer one.

I enjoyed everything about *The Dream*. Then at the weekends Godfrey asked us all to the Welcombe and we had sociable meals and amused each other. There was Robert Shaw, of course, and Edmund Purdom, whom Godfrey was very taken with (he said he was so cheeky), and Robert Hardy – Godfrey liked him the best. Robert has talked to me about that season, and he remembers the first time he met Godfrey. It was in the dimly-lit stalls while he was watching a rehearsal and a tall figure loomed up and sat down beside him. A voice you couldn't mistake murmured, "Tearle."

Deeply impressed, Robert muttered, "How do you do, Sir."

During a pause in the rehearsal, Godfrey said in a friendly way,

"Like to see a picture of my girl friend?"

Fascinated, Robert waited.

Godfrey took out his wallet, and showed him a photograph of his boat.

Three

The young actors knew Godfrey well now, and they had all adopted the nickname I had given him to bridge the gap between star and walk-on. "Are you lunching with God today?" people would ask each other. Or, "Any sign of God about?" Godfrey liked his elevation to the deity but was not so keen on the other version of the name, Old God. Robert Hardy gave himself a matching name, he was Goosegod.

Robert Hardy, like Robert Shaw and Edmund Purdom, had become a friend. He was clever, classically good looking, and determined to succeed. But unlike his friend Robert Shaw, with whom at one time he shared a house in the country outside Stratford, he didn't think that acting was a head-on attack in which you merely used your personality. He was already becoming a subtle actor, and in the following year took quite important parts at Stratford and did well. He and I were not close friends, though, until years later when I was playing in London with Gladys Cooper, and Robert was about to marry her daughter Sally. Then all four of us saw a lot of each other.

The past is a panorama with bits missing. Some of it is in vivid and unfading colours, parts are a dull monochrome, and then you come across odd inexplicable blanks. Like frescoes painted on damp walls containing mineral salts, the pictures have flaked and faded to be lost for ever. I wonder if you remember clearly only what most strongly affects you? Or is that too simple, and is it that there are times when you are in a particularly receptive state, and what happens *then* remains somewhere in your mind and can be called back into heartbreaking reality? Did it rain that summer? I don't remember it doing so. I recall nothing but hot sunny days, and tall grasses and weeds on either side of the Warwickshire lanes when Godfrey and I drove out into the country. The french windows of his rooms at the Welcombe hotel always seemed to be wide open on to the garden.

I liked him and I loved him. He was easy, mysterious and arrogant; he had an almost American glamour. In fact his mother had been American, and on her side he was a quarter Jewish. He said that was the best part of him. "You must pretend to be a quarter Jewish," he said to me once. "It's quite a plus."

When he was with me and the other young members of the company he was amusing and relaxed. He seemed to be much younger and braver and funnier than the boys I knew, all of whom were busy worrying about why they were not playing the First Gentleman, just as I was worrying about why I was not playing the First Fairy.

Yet there were times when I did feel conscious of Godfrey's age; it would have been stupid of me to pretend otherwise. Once on a very hot Sunday we decided, after lunch at the Welcombe, that we all wanted to go swimming. The only open-air swimming pool was outside Stratford, so we piled into two or three cars and drove off. On the journey, sitting by Godfrey with the long summer afternoon ahead, I was suddenly and unexpectedly aware that Godfrey really was much older than us. I thought – perhaps he's too old to enjoy swimming after a large lunch. I felt bothered. I went off with some girl friends when we arrived, to change into my swimsuit. It was before the fashion for bikinis and my suit was black – to cover up my ageing puppy fat – and expensive. I'd had compliments about it. When we came out of the changing room to the edge of the pool, Godfrey was already there. He had changed into very brief burgundy-coloured trunks. Without his clothes he looked more than ever like a gorilla, he was covered with hair. He climbed up to the top diving board, stood for a moment, and then dived in without a ripple. He swam one length, climbed out of the water and rolled a cigarette. Nobody wanted to swim much after that.

Godfrey was only in two of the season's plays. The first was *Macbeth* and the second a revival later in the season of his previous year's great success, *Othello*. He had also been offered the role of Wolsey in Tyrone Guthrie's *Henry VIII* which was coming into the repertory as the final play, and had agreed to do it. But Anthony Quayle decided to take the company to Australia when the season ended, and Godfrey now found that the role and the tour seemed to go together. *Henry VIII* was possibly going to be one of the plays to travel. Godfrey decided against it. He didn't want to tour Australia or anywhere else – all that was in the past for him. But he was deeply disappointed, for he wanted very much to play Wolsey. He told me he would have done so "showing Wolsey as the butcher he was".

So with *Macbeth* as the only play in which Godfrey was at present appearing, he found having so many days when he did not work a bore, despite our companionship and his many visitors. He drove to London sometimes to spend his free days, took up his bachelor life, played bridge at the Garrick and went to the theatre. When he came back after one London visit he told me he'd seen James Bridie's new play, *Daphne Laureola*, with Edith Evans, Felix Aylmer and "a new young actor called Peter Finch who's having a big success. He's very good indeed." Godfrey spoke with that particular appreciation which always sounded in his voice when he talked about talent. Godfrey took the opportunity, when he was in London, to see a number of his friends. I think he found people of his own age a distinct relief.

A new play had come into the repertory, the not-often-performed *Cymbeline*. Although it was directed by Michael Benthall, I was just a court lady who stood about in medieval poses with one hip stuck out. There was nothing to be done with a walking-on part except to look and move well. But I had something new and worrying to occupy my thoughts. *Othello* was hoving into view.

Othello had been Godfrey's own production the previous year and, as I've said, a great success. In his last season as director, Barry Jackson had asked Godfrey to Stratford. Jackson also adored the talented young and it was he who had hired the young Peter Brook, Paul Scofield and Michael Benthall; the Memorial Theatre teemed with very clever and very young people. "But they'd better be careful," Jackson said when Godfrey agreed to come, "or they're going to find they've got someone who will swamp them all." *Othello* almost did that. Here, said the *Guardian*, was Othello as Shakespeare saw him and meant him to be. "The noblest and clearest piece of Shakespearean acting I've ever seen." I was to play Bianca. This was my chance, my thirty-seven speaking lines. I wasn't a walk-on or a fairy, a small boy or an apparition. I was a real woman . . . and here was the snag. Weeks ago when we first became friends, Godfrey had told me he did not approve of my being chosen for the part. He himself, with Anthony Quayle, had cast most of the leading players. But it was while Godfrey had been away in America that Anthony Quayle had given me Bianca and made a place for me in the season.

Godfrey took me out to lunch expressly to tell me he didn't think I was right for the part.

"It's better to tell you this now," he said. "Then we can work at it together."

If any other director in the world had coolly informed me before rehearsals began that he considered me entirely unsuited to the part I was going to play, I would have had a fit of the shakes. I still would today. But Godfrey was calm and kind. We would, as he said, work at it together.

Despite my concentrated work, despite all Godfrey's skill and patience, I never did get that Venetian bauble right. Bianca is a whore and Cassio is her customer. She drags about the streets after him, she loudly declares her hope that he will marry her. At such an absurd idea, Cassio simply laughs. Bianca is for sale, not for respectability. I was wrong for the part. I hadn't the knowledge, the instinct, the experience or the sexual security. I did not even look right. I was better as Fleance than as Bianca, better as Fairy Fraught; at least I moved well. The costume for Bianca had been designed for another girl, Heather Stannard, who had played the part the previous year. She was dark and voluptuous and the costume was in glowing reds and black. As for the wig, when I put it on I knew I could never, never wear it. I looked dreadful. My kind dresser comforted me and before the dress rehearsal she did my own hair in big curls. For the rest of the season, she got to the theatre especially early to give herself time to do my hair for me; I was so grateful.

There were surprises during the *Othello* rehearsals. One of the Moor's group of soldiers was played by Michael Bates, a wonderfully gifted character actor who later became famous on television as a comedian. Anthony Quayle took Godfrey aside and objected to Michael being a mere trooper. Michael, he said, had been an officer in the Gurkhas during the war. He must be raised to the rank of officer for *Othello*.

Godfrey had made cuts in the play the previous year – most notably he removed the epilepsy scene when Othello falls down groaning and foaming at the mouth. The purists had been horrified – you could not just take out a vital piece of Othello's character in that arbitrary way. Godfrey was unmoved. He didn't like the scene; it didn't fit with *his* concept of Othello. Fifty years before, his father, Osmond Tearle, a superb actor-manager of his time, hadn't liked it either. As Osmond had done, Godfrey cut the scene. He wrote a generous letter to *The Times* saying that Anthony Quayle had only agreed to the cut under protest; it was entirely his – Godfrey's – responsibility.

The public adored him in *Othello*. At every per-formance they cheered and simply would not let him go.

I did work at Bianca, but the part didn't work for me and Godfrey never pretended that it did. Once during the rehearsal, after my big scene, he said pityingly,

"It would be better if you came on with a hockey stick."

The curious thing was that when he was sarcastic it never hurt me. The content of his voice was not vicious. But I hated playing Bianca; dread entered my heart every evening when the play was on. I knew I was inept and I knew Godfrey thought so. He used to stand in the wings while I played my scene, when Cassio gives Bianca Desdemona's handkerchief and she becomes furiously jealous. As Othello, Godfrey wore a long white robe like a nightdress, which made him look even larger and taller. There he stood, watch-ing me. I wanted to sink into the ground. I was quite brave to bear it, but I was not frightened of him. He wasn't a bully.

I have written about my small part, which to me then was something large and worrying, and have not said anything about Godfrey's performance. He showed you a man of enormous dignity, a very soph-isticated man, not a savage. This impression never broke, even in the jealousy scenes. Bernard Shaw says that the jealousy scenes in *Othello* are music, that they are abstract. "The words do not convey ideas: they are streaming ensigns and tossing branches to make the tempest of passion visible." And Shaw adds that the actor "must have the orchestral quality in him and that is a matter largely of physical endowment". That was what Godfrey had. He used his voice to make an abstract music which was extraordinarily powerful and affecting. He was not realistic when he was cut to the heart with jealousy, and the effect was the stronger because the man did not go to pieces. Suffering, he never broke. The epilepsy scene would never have been right for such an interpretation. Godfrey's presence as Othello was full of power. He was a patrician. I remember how I was struck by the way he could listen. He stood still, his eyes fixed on the actor speaking to him, and listened intently, absorbedly. Other actors of his generation used to switch off and simply stand waiting for their turn to speak again. It was Godfrey who taught me how to listen onstage.

I always watched the end of the play. The tears rolled down his face as he said the last speech,

> Of one not easily jealous, but, being wrought,
> Perplex'd in the extreme;

He never talked about the performance afterwards and once when we were together after the play I suddenly asked,

"What *were* you thinking about tonight in the last scene?"

"What I was going to have for supper."

It wasn't true.

After *Othello* came into the repertory and was given the same tremendous notices as the previous year, my mother telephoned to say she would like to come and see the play. Would I arrange a seat for her? I wished she had not chosen *Othello*, but since she was such an admirer of Godfrey's the only other play she would wish to see would be *Macbeth*. I was not sure which of the two I wanted her to see me in less . . . Bianca or Fleance? There was also another far greater reason for worrying about her visit. I hadn't told her about Godfrey.

I was utterly devoted to my mother. I was an only child, born in Penang where my father had with considerable success built up a merchant firm and owned rubber plantations. My mother lived in colonial style and was very spoiled. She had been horrified when she found she was pregnant. She was in her late forties and her friends had begun to be grandparents – and here was she, having a baby. She was not even at my christening: she had arranged to play polo.

As can happen when a woman has a baby late in life, we became unusually close. We had been, so to speak, flung unexpectedly together, and I grew out of babyhood quickly. When the war came our life changed utterly. My father was taken prisoner and was in a Japanese prisoner-of-war camp for nearly five years. My mother managed to get me and herself back to England. We lived in hotels. So many hotels that they are still home to me. Going through my own front door is fine, but I always feel more at home at the Connaught.

I had been putting off telling my mother about Godfrey because I minded what *she* thought more than anybody else in the world. I dreaded the idea that she would disapprove – and how could she not? With understated irony, Godfrey himself had said we were "scarcely ideal". The more I thought about my mother's arrival in Stratford, the more daunted I became. The two most important people in my life were going to meet, and what would happen?

"It's much the best for us to meet each other," Godfrey had said. Was it? And what ought I to tell her beforehand?

Godfrey was already in the theatre by the time she arrived from the London train. I only had a moment to kiss her, and fix for us to see each other after the matinee, then I had to dash across the road from the Arden to change into Bianca's red and black, and have my hair curled.

Farce comes into one's life at completely unexpected moments. I had been worrying about my mother's visit for days. I had wondered how to break the news – how to begin. But as things turned out, I could have saved myself a lot of agonising.

I mentioned earlier that the tables in the Arden dining room were placed very close together. The room was not very large. It was quite impossible to avoid hearing any conversation going on at the next table, supposing that one happened to be eating alone. The first name my mother heard when she sat down to lunch was mine.

Sitting at the next table, also having lunch before the matinee, were Dorothy Hyson, Anthony Quayle's wife, and her mother the musical comedy actress Dorothy Dickson. Both looked attractive and spirited and were thoroughly enjoying a gossip.

"Godfrey Tearle," they agreed, "has definitely gone mad. He's chasing about with some slip of a girl called Jill Bennett."

There was a lot more of this, and although they were enjoying the chat they were very disapproving. Even shocked.

When the performance was over I changed hurriedly and came across the road to the Arden. I had already told my mother that Godfrey was coming to have tea with us, and she'd looked surprised and pleased. Now, when I came into the lounge where she was waiting and sat down beside her she said at once, drily,

"It seems, Jill, that you're being disapproved of."

And told me what she had heard.

I didn't know what to say. I simply hadn't imagined that Godfrey and I together would shock people, that we were being discussed and criticised. I hadn't even considered he was too old. I just thought him the most glamorous of men and that I was having a whirling, wonderful summer. I sat and looked at her, feeling frightened.

Just then, Godfrey arrived. He walked into the Arden lounge with that swaying, lithe, gorilla's walk which was so much part of him, and came up to be introduced. My mother and he did look good together. She was not unlike Katharine Hepburn: she had the same racehorse look, the flared nostrils and long neck. She was rather shy when they met and seemed haughty, which is something I'm told that I do.

During tea I said almost nothing. They were pleasant to each other, of course, and the only way I can describe how Godfrey was is to say that he was full of care. It must have been very difficult for him – he and I could have lost everything. He was very loving about me, but he was gentle to my mother. Somehow he made it seem possible and my mother, herself younger than Godfrey, managed to see that. She was imaginative and she saw how safe we were about each other. She also knew I was headstrong and must be left to make my own mistakes.

She liked him very much. He had a strong fascinating personality, and you couldn't help being drawn to him. But whether she liked the idea of Godfrey and me together was another matter. The very word "couple" for us, for the legendary actor and the beginner,

seemed ridiculous. She was too realistic to make it
hard for us, but she had vision as Godfrey had. She
knew I was in for a lot of sadness in the end.

I was much too nervous during tea to ask her what
she had thought of my performance. And I didn't
think I wanted to know either; it would be certain to be
the same as Godfrey's opinion. I was right. When she
did mention it later she was unimpressed and disappointed. But civilised about it.

The season was in full swing now. The town was busy
with visitors at weekends, but during the week it had
the look and feel of a university town. The actors went
about on bicycles with baskets filled with books, and
left their bicycles trustingly unpadlocked in rows at
the stage door, as if parked outside a college. For one
to be stolen was quite a rarity. We spent our afternoons, when there were no matinees, on the river.
Julian Amyes, who was in his twenties, was playing
the elderly Friar in *Much Ado*. He used to time it
perfectly, step straight off a punt, go into the theatre,
put on his monk's cassock and appear in the fourth act,
when Claudio rejects Hero.

We went to picnics. We went to parties. We larked
about. The office of John Goodwin, the theatre's publi-
cist, was not far from the dressing-rooms, and he told
me recently that one evening he met me dashing down
the corridor, wearing a big straw hat, and without a
stitch on. I don't remember that. I'm sure Godfrey
would *not* have approved.

On some evenings we were invited to parties given
at the British Council. Their Stratford home at that
time was at Mason Croft, which had once belonged to
the romantic late Victorian and early Edwardian
novelist Marie Corelli. It was a glorious fifteenth-
century house, but it had been a dilapidated wreck

when she bought it in 1901. She rescued and renovated it, and wrote her books in the Elizabethan watch tower in the garden.

We went to a party in her music room, where her initials could still be seen carved over the fireplace. I loved the stories about her. She was passionate about Stratford, made her permanent home there, went about saving Tudor cottages from being demolished, gave Christmas parties at the theatre. Best of all, she startled Stratford very much when in 1903 she decided she found driving about in her carriage too noisy and dusty. She sent to Venice for a gondola, and what's more, engaged a real Italian gondolier. She said no English boatman would be able to propel a gondola in the right way. Her gondola was called *The Dream*, and people called *her* the modern Swan of Avon. American visitors enjoyed seeing her floating by as much as – even more than – visiting Shakespeare's birthplace.

Stratford in 1949 had not changed all that much from the Warwickshire market town she had known. It was still countryfied, and the actors and directors loved working in such an enchanting place. The town, though, rather resented the arrival of these famous people. In the past they had only read about them, and now here they were sauntering about Stratford streets as if they owned the place.

I was still in the same digs near the theatre and still being patronised by my landlady and her daughter. I had proved a disappointment by playing such small roles. They were very taken aback once when I had flu, and Godfrey called to ask after me. The sight of this famous man standing in their hallway thoroughly put them out. They did not know what to make of it.

"May I," said Godfrey with all his charm, "bring her some food?"

He had Fortnum's in mind.

Drawing herself up, my landlady snapped,

"Certainly not."

I had to convalesce on plums and custard instead of
petits fours and peaches in brandy. But as I did not
hear until later that there had been a choice, I didn't
miss them.

When I was better, Godfrey drove me out for more
country expeditions. We rarely walked. I didn't know
it, but Godfrey had had a thrombosis in his leg and it
hurt him to walk even a short distance. He never
mentioned that to me, and it never affected his work
onstage where he moved as easily as a dancer. Once
we did go for a walk through Stratford; we were on our
way to the library to change his book. Godfrey had to
stop – his leg had become very painful. It was the first
time I knew about it and, something he never did, he
swore. He was furious with himself. We never got as
far as the library. I went alone.

Very late in the season Tyrone Guthrie arrived in
Stratford; a patrician figure, astonishingly tall and
thin, with piercing eyes; he was like a popular slightly
scratchy schoolmaster. Before his arrival he sent a
telegram to Anthony Quayle: "Ask Dot to hire for us a
covered punt." Dorothy Hyson managed to find one;
it had a hooped canvas cover to keep off the rain.
During his stay in Stratford, Tyrone Guthrie lived in
the punt, together with his wife Judy who was nearly
as tall as he was. Apparently they were perfectly
comfortable, the punt being the right length for two
thin giants. They punted to the theatre in the mornings, tied up, and in the evenings punted back slowly
up river to their anchorage.

This year at Stratford Guthrie was directing *Henry
VIII* with Anthony Quayle as the king and Diana
Wynyard as Katharine of Aragon. Guthrie was a considerable figure in the theatre. There was no one
among the great names whom he hadn't directed, at
one time or another, at the Vic. Rather as Peter Brook's

work is talked about now, Guthrie's was – with bated breath. He would have disliked that if he'd overheard. He once said he wanted his work to be remembered only by a few and for a while, with warmth and joy, or else totally forgotten. He preferred to write on water.

Most of the junior members of the company were afraid of him, but I never was. Anthony Quayle and John Gielgud alarmed me much more. Guthrie worked with complete openness, he never took an actor on one side to mutter suggestions or criticisms, he simply shouted from the stalls, "That won't do!" Or used his famous phrase, "Never mind, dear, astonish us in the morning."

He was an extrovert and a bit of a genius. Kenneth Tynan wrote, "Unleash him on Shakespeare and the result will be catastrophically brilliant". Guthrie liked pageantry and banners, high drama and ludicrous anti-climax. He made *Henry VIII* very funny. Court gentlemen went on country walks across the stage, climbed invisible stiles and avoided imaginary cow pats. The feast given by Wolsey was turned into a debauch, courtiers were sick and girls fainted. He moved his actors in swirling patterns and if he thought the plot was slowing down he upset a throne, or somebody sneezed during a high-flown speech. Guthrie's grandfather had been a general, and he himself was educated at the military college at Wellington. Since he liked filling the stage with crowds, he borrowed fourteen soldiers from the Royal Warwickshire Regiment for *Henry VIII*.

Anthony Quayle's Henry VIII had short red hair. He was strong and vigorous, with a lust for life, and a very political king. You never doubted that what he wanted he was going to get.

I felt like a real actress when Guthrie directed me. He was well known for giving unexpected moments to the small part actors and walk-ons, and he gave me a lot of walking alone across the stage. And a dance all to myself. The leading actors did not exactly enjoy the time and trouble he took with the walk-ons; he treated us like stars. It was our turn to have a good time.

Of course there were dramas and the biggest was when Guthrie sacked Edmund Purdom after the first night. Everybody liked Edmund, he was so good natured and such good company, and wonderfully knowledgeable about music. He was absurdly handsome, with an olive skin and thick glossy hair. Edmund only had a tiny part in *Henry VIII*, but on the first night he missed his entrance. We were all horror struck and intrigued. How *could* an actor miss his entrance on a first night? Where had he been? It seemed Edmund had been in the Wardrobe, machining a pair of satin knickers as a present for Heather Stannard, with whom he was madly in love.

When Guthrie sacked him, some of the high-ups in the company pleaded for Edmund. Couldn't he be given another chance? Guthrie was adamant. "Don't worry about Purdom," he said. "He'll be a star or he'll sink without trace." Three years later Edmund went to Hollywood, and was given the full star treatment.

All the plays were in the repertory now – six, and I was in every one of them. On one evening I would wear Mariano Andreu's green and white robes in *Much Ado*, on another Fleance's fur and bole, on another I would have to face the ordeal of Godfrey's great baleful eyes in *Othello*. To be part of a theatre company is to become a member of a temporary family, and I knew and enjoyed that. Yet I spent all my free time with Godfrey and that cut me off from being close to people of my own age. They were all taken up by now with high romances, or they were worrying about their careers. As for me, I found acting with Godfrey made me restless. Here I was onstage with a real actor, a genius. All that did was make me thirst to do more.

Godfrey told me that I must persevere, that he knew I really had something. He was truly encouraging. He gave me a life of Henry Irving, and wrote in it, "In the bright lexicon of fate which youth preserves, there's no such word as Fail."*

I swung from being happy with Godfrey to being deeply dissatisfied with myself. He knew how I felt. Among the things I learned from him was how to conduct myself in the curious life I'd chosen. Because an actor must nerve himself to pass many tests. When you try for a part, the director may decide against you for reasons as basic as that you're simply too young or too old, too fat or too thin. Then he may think you too stylish or too homely, too clever or too slow. Any of these things, and scores more, can count against you. So you must learn to brace yourself to bear that harsh analysis, hold on to your quality and never become second rate. You have to survive. If love is like being thrown about in a rough sea, so is acting.

Godfrey understood my anxieties; he had his sombre side too. In all the time that I knew him, he never once sent me a telegram wishing me luck. What he wished for me was happiness. I have always been given to Celtic gloom: my father was Scots and my great-great-uncle was Henry Campbell Bannerman, who was Prime Minister of the Liberal government from 1906 to his death in 1908. I have Campbell blood. They're a strange lot the Campbells; they have to get used to the burden of the past. I was at school for a while in Ballachulish, and a number of the girls there were Macdonalds. In my simplicity, I told them that I was a Campbell. The revelation was greeted with horror. After two hundred and fifty years, they were still wincing from the pain of Glencoe.

* Actually what Bulwer-Lytton wrote in *Richelieu* was: "In the lexicon of youth which Fate reserves/For a bright manhood, there is no such word/As – *fail!* . . ."

In spite of the fun we were having during the season, in spite of – even because – the place where I was working was beautiful, most of all in spite of having a marvellous companion, I actually wanted the season to end. Godfrey thought it comic when I said this, and I often did.

One Sunday evening when we were having dinner in the country, he suddenly said,

"I've been thinking that I'll give a flashy party at the end of the season."

I was delighted.

"We'll have fireworks," he added.

For a joyful moment I thought he had guessed how much I liked them. Of course I couldn't help asking,

"Why fireworks?"

"Diana likes them." He gave me a teasing look, guessing my conceited thought.

One by one, we gave the last performances of the plays. Tyrone Guthrie once wrote that most performances are forgotten by audiences in a matter of hours or weeks. A few last for years, a very few for generations. For actors, too, a performance vanishes leaving no trace and only a few remain imprinted on his imagination. I remember one or two of the characters I have played, sometimes uneasily because the part was important to me, and I still feel as if, when it ended, I lost a piece of myself. For a while, anyway.

The last performance of a play has a certain poignancy for the actors as well as the audience. It is curious to look at your own face in the dressing-room glass before you go on, and realise that *that* person staring at you, transformed, will soon be gone for ever.

But there wasn't any feeling of regret or wonder for me when the last night of *Macbeth* arrived. I was filled with relish. It was very selfish of me to feel like that, since this had been the play which meant so much to Godfrey and had haunted him for years, finally proving such a bitter disappointment. But an actor must be selfish, or how can he work at all? I had hated my role of Fleance when we began to rehearse in February, and now in October I hated it just as steadily. I enjoyed one scene, the fight in the dark and the defying of Macbeth, but for the rest – I couldn't bear playing a young boy and now I was not going to do it any more.

The last performance ended to terrific applause and I ran up to my dressing-room so excited at the thought that it was over – at last it was over! – that I took hold of my costume and tore it to shreds. Everything. The leggings. The jacket. The fur. There was a clever, sharp little man in the Wardrobe, Jacky Wilson, who was very kind to me, and after I had committed the fell deed I gathered up the remains of Fleance, which now looked like a dead cat, carried it to Jacky and confessed. He raised his pencilled eyebrows and grinned.

I don't know why Godfrey chose Ettington Park for his party. I expect because of its size, and the fact that there was a ballroom where we could all dance. The hotel had been the home of the Shirley family and in those days it looked as if it still was. There is something very curious about the building. Actually it was a seventeenth-century mansion which Victorian architects didn't pull down but repaired. Then they encased the whole building in brown and ochre-coloured stone, adding pinnacles like those of a French château. There is this high Victorian building, yet it has a feeling of a much much older house, and in the garden is a ruined church where some of the Shirleys are buried. When we arrived at Ettington Park it was already dark, and we felt the Shirleys were just about to appear at the party, risen up from the church nearby. Down the end of a dark passage you'd be certain to meet one of them.

The haunted grange effect added to the success of the party. It was crowded with everybody from the theatre. It was typical of Godfrey in days of sharp divisions in what was certainly *not* a classless theatre that he had invited everybody, from the stars to the walk-ons, from the directors to the youngest musician and the girl who was doing some part-time sewing in the Wardrobe. There were well over a hundred of us flooding in through the high-ceilinged rooms. Everybody was happy and excited – theatre people are like that at parties. It was the fashion for dresses to be very rich and bare-shouldered, and all the girls had naked shoulders and wide sweeping skirts. I had had a special dress made by a friend in the Wardrobe, Ray Diffin. It was very bizarre, green and gold in tiers.

There was a sit-down supper first. Godfrey had asked me whom I wanted to sit next to and I had chosen Michael Gwynn. He was a tall, thin, clever actor, an intellectual, very gentle and beautiful and I admired him.

After the meal there were speeches and Godfrey was presented with a sword – the sword he had used in *Macbeth*. We all applauded and laughed, because we thought we might cry. Godfrey made a graceful speech in reply, he was good at that, and said that he would always treasure the sword. I suppose he did, in his way. When we were in London the following winter he used it as a poker for the fire. It was extremely heavy and always lay in the hearth.

After the speeches we danced, then a big space was made on the ballroom floor and we played noisy musical chairs, plumping down on each other's laps instead of the chairs. We danced again. Godfrey had told me before the party that he wasn't going to dance. If I had been more imaginative I would have remembered that he had been in pain with his leg. Besides, if he danced with me, he would have to dance with a lot of other people. I didn't think of that. I was excited by the party and the music and the noise, and most of all by the fact that everything was ending. I *wanted* him to dance with me. I wanted to show my power over him, I suppose – it was the nasty side of my character. So I coaxed and he agreed. He did dance with me, beautifully too, but he was not at all pleased and he showed it. I don't think I ever forced Godfrey to do anything he did not want to do again.

Finally, it was very late, we crowded out into the grounds in the damp autumn night to watch "Diana's fireworks" as Godfrey called them. There were rockets and Catherine wheels and silver rain, and those fireworks which fly up and then leave one suspended blue star slowly floating down behind the trees. Years later Ralph Richardson said the best thing about these sparkling temporary joys.

"I love fireworks," he said. "They're so unnecessary."

The next morning Godfrey was leaving Stratford.

"I'll see you soon," he said. And gave me his wink. He drove away from Stratford. He never played there again.

It wasn't good after Godfrey had gone. I missed my friend, and the theatre seemed so dull and the last days of the season an anti-climax. People in the company talked about nothing but whether they were going to be asked back to play in next year's season. Backstage there were anxious faces everywhere. I knew I was not going to be asked – that was obvious. Anyway, I thought, I was too young to have been in the A.T.S. during the war and, with our director, heroes were popular.

Yet in spite of my grumbling and frustration, I had been a member of a big company, and all my decisions this year had been made for me. From now on I had to start a very different life. I must face reality.

It was already October and the air in Stratford smelled of bonfires. The thick Virginia creeper which coated the walls of the old part of the theatre had begun to turn a deep shiny red. When I had packed, and said goodbye to my landlady and given her a final sweet ration, I went to the theatre to say goodbye to friends. They had been part of every day since I had first walked into the rehearsal room nine months ago. I might not see them again for a long time. Perhaps never.

I went out of the stage door. The river was still, and the arches of the old tramway bridge were reflected in it, a line of circles instead of hoops. On an impulse, I went into the picture gallery, walked up the stairs and stood looking at the portrait of Godfrey's father, Osmond Tearle, as Lear.

Godfrey had taken me to see the painting during the summer.

"That's my father," he had said. "He was the greatest actor I've ever seen. And he's the reason I can never play Lear. I still remember the way he spoke the five 'nevers'."

I stood for a while, but I wasn't thinking about Osmond Tearle. The gallery was deserted, except for me and the famous actors on the walls. Garrick and Sarah Siddons, Kean and Fanny Kemble. Some of them stared fixedly down at me with huge eyes, some looked away, deep in their roles. What have I achieved since I've been here? I wondered. And then I thought that Stratford had been worthwhile. Because of Godfrey.

But I was glad to walk down the stairs, turn my back on the theatre and walk briskly to the station.

Four

While we were in Stratford, Godfrey had often talked about his house in Cornwall. He had lived in Cornwall on and off for years, and loved it. He was more than just attracted to a beautiful place which he'd discovered by chance. Godfrey told me that he always felt it was *his* county; he had Cornish blood on his father's side, and he felt completely at home there. It was the place he wanted to be. But I found out later that he didn't mean he would live permanently there.

After his farewell party when *Othello* ended, Godfrey went straight from Stratford down to Cornwall. He had already asked me if I would like to join him when the season was over, and I had accepted at once. The idea of a real holiday with Godfrey sounded wonderful. I travelled down to Cornwall in a luxurious first-class sleeper – steam in those days. Godfrey had sent me my ticket.

I had been to Cornwall once before when I was a child; my grandmother lived in a rambling old country house in Devon and on one holiday during the war, instead of taking me to stay with her, my mother decided that she and I would go to Cornwall. We stayed – as always – in a hotel; she never took furnished cottages. All I remember of that holiday now was a lot of sea. In keeping with this simple thought, Godfrey met my train wearing a pair of thigh-length sea boots. I'm sure he had dressed up on purpose. He looked magnificent.

"Come along," he said, "I want you to see my house."

He had described the house, which was at Messack

Point in St. Just-in-Roseland, a tiny village on a creek of the Carrick Roads. He'd explained that "roads" meant a piece of sheltered water near a shore, handy as a harbour. Now we set off in Godfrey's car through rough lonely country. We crossed stretches of moorland and I saw glimpses of the sea shining in the distance. Finally he turned up a cart track which was so rough that it made the car bounce and shudder. And then, there was the house.

It wasn't at all what I had imagined. I had thought of it as either a fisherman's cottage or a manor house, even a mixture of both. But Godfrey's house was solid and simple and exactly like a child's drawing of a house, square, with squares for windows and an oblong for a door; there was even smoke coming out of the chimney. The garden was nothing much but lawns, a few weedy flower beds and some young trees which Godfrey had planted. I've always liked people who plant trees. It's a sign of a generous nature.

A pleasant married couple, the man was called Charles, welcomed me without surprise, taking my presence for granted. One of Charles's main jobs was looking after the boat; his wife kept house and did the cooking.

Godfrey couldn't wait to take me to the bay where his boat was moored. I'd been curious to see the house and was even more interested to see the boat, the girl friend whose picture he'd shown to Robert Hardy. We went down a rocky path to the beach. The shingle was wet from the retreating tide. We looked across the water.

"I won't row you out until later. You need your breakfast first. I just wanted you to take a look at her."

The boat, a thirty-two-foot cutter, was worth looking at. She was large and graceful, her tall mast rocked gently in the swell. She was named *Barbara Mary*, after Godfrey's third (and last) wife.

69

Later during the holiday he suggested that he might change the name.

"What do you think? To *Jill* perhaps?"

"No."

He looked at me.

"You're right. We don't need things like that."

During supper that evening Godfrey told me that while he'd been married to Barbara Mary he had first come to live in Cornwall. He talked about her very little, but I had the impression that she was attractive and had a strong character. She and Godfrey eventually parted; there was a divorce and she married again, first to a clergyman who died and then to another who became a bishop.

It was early in the last war that she suggested that he might like to give up acting and move down to Cornwall. He'd always wanted to live there, so why not do it now? Godfrey certainly was not persuaded against his will to the decision, he was never a man who could be talked into things. In fact, he always got his own way – in the end. But he was attracted to his wife's idea. It was a dramatic thing to do, and actors are irresistibly drawn to the big gesture. It would be such a change; it might be a new lease of life after so many years of theatre and films.

He was playing at the time in a big success, Emlyn Williams's *The Light of Heart*, and the critics had said Godfrey was giving one of his best performances for years. He played a strong tragic role, that of a great theatre star of the past who had ruined his career by drink. All he does now is to play Father Christmas at the local bazaar. Then the unbelievable chance comes – he's asked to play Lear. It is the role which (like Godfrey's own passion to play Macbeth) the drunken actor has always longed for. He gives up drink. And at the dress rehearsal gives a superb performance. But final success at the first night escapes him. He starts to drink again – from exhilaration, nerves, everything.

When Emlyn Williams learned that Godfrey had really made up his mind to leave the play, he did a very Emlyn Williams thing. He sat down and re-wrote the part for a younger man – for himself.

"And so," Godfrey said, "the character I'd played, the father who wanted to play Lear, became the brother whose ambition was to play Hamlet. Angela Baddeley had been my daughter. She became the sister."

He told me this in the matter-of-fact tone of an actor who accepts one of the hazards of his job – that he is replaceable. However great the actor is, another can be found who is as good, or nearly as good. It is a salutary thing to remember.

But the fact that Godfrey decided to stop acting did seem to me to be very astonishing.

"What did you *do?*" I wanted to know.

He bought a large house on the Helford river and started to lead a Cornish life. He and Barbara Mary enjoyed being in the country; they met the local big-wigs and interested themselves in what Godfrey called "the Duchy". He didn't talk to his Cornish friends about acting. They discussed local matters on which he soon became an expert.

Certainly Godfrey felt deeply about Cornwall and from that time on always looked on it as his home. Cornish people maintain that their county has a physical separateness from England. Some Cornish-men say they can sense it directly they cross the river Tamar. A. L. Rowse has written that whenever he arrives back in Cornwall, he feels that he ought to show his passport. Godfrey had a deep affection and understanding for Cornwall. He was thinking of it when he used his favourite description of himself, "I come from yeoman stock." But I have an idea that he never exactly wanted to stay permanently – the gypsy and the Cornishman in him didn't mesh. Or perhaps he did intend to remain in Cornwall when he first made his home there. He was obsessed by the sea, and couldn't have inherited a county to love which was closer to the sea. In its whole length, and Cornwall is very big, the sea is never more than twenty miles away. Usually you can see it in the distance. Or you know it's just over that nearby hill.

Godfrey and Barbara Mary's house had gardens leading down to the beach. I suppose he must have sailed with the friends he made locally, and this revived his love of sailing. He'd sailed with his father when he was a boy. But he didn't yet buy himself a boat.

He fitted comfortably into the county. J. C. Trewin tells the story of a local taxi driver, when Godfrey was living near Helford, who said to him, "Mr. Tearle lives near here, you know. A perfect gentleman. You wouldn't think that he was an actor."

The way Godfrey described his previous life in Cornwall made me think he had spent a considerable time there. But his retirement (how can an actor retire? He goes on acting all his life) was short-lived. Godfrey was scarcely settled in his life as a country gentleman when his old colleague Michael Powell telephoned.

"I'm making a new film and I'm quite excited about it. It's about the R.A.F. Called *One of Our Aircraft is Missing*. I've been wondering if I might persuade you to play the navigator."

He went on to describe Godfrey's part in the tempting manner that directors use when they are trying to get actors to join them.

There had been a lot of offers before Michael Powell's. Godfrey turned them down. He didn't bother to tell me about them – he never talked about parts he had decided against. But this film, the part, and Michael Powell himself, all attracted him. Powell was extremely difficult and very creative to work with. He was clever with his leading actors, too. Knowing about Godfrey's love of Cornwall he finished the conversation with a surprise.

"Suppose," he said, "instead of a salary we gave you a boat?"

Godfrey accepted.

"Were you pleased at going back to work?" I asked.

"Relieved," said Godfrey with candour.

And that was the history of the *Barbara Mary*.

I wasn't allowed to hang about at Messack Point over breakfast the next morning. I was hurried, clumping, down the rocky path dressed in full Cornish seaman's gear. Godfrey had bought it for me before I arrived. There were thick oiled wool sweaters, oilskins, stout gumboots and a real sou'wester. I looked like an old-fashioned advertisement for Halibut Liver Oil.

He rowed me out to the *Barbara Mary* in the dinghy, and we climbed on board. I hadn't set foot on deck two minutes before I found that my role had changed. I was no longer the welcomed guest, the girl he was fond of and whom he enjoyed spoiling and chatting to, the one who made him laugh. I was the cabin boy (a role I was later to play in the Alan Ladd film *Hell Below Zero*).

Godfrey rapped out instructions as he hoisted the sails, looked across at me and expected me to jump to it. I was given the job of sluicing the deck with a mop. I got rather good at being cabin boy after a while. There seemed a lot of housework to do on that boat during the holidays. I loved doing it in a boat as much as I loathed it in a house. It might be Charles's job to look after the boat, but Godfrey *liked* everything to do with the *Barbara Mary* and wanted me to like it too. So I washed the deck, and polished the woodwork until it was so bright it looked positively vulgar.

When we set off to sail up river my role changed again; I was ordered to put away the mop and become first mate. I'd sailed a bit in Cornwall as a child, and also on a loch when I was at school in Scotland, but I'd forgotten everything I knew, including every word of the vocabulary. I didn't know that a rope was a sheet, I had no idea what the painter was, and I was inclined to argue.

"Never argue with the Captain," snapped Godfrey.

He wasn't joking.

The autumn gales had begun in Cornwall and it often poured with rain. These were the equinoctial gales which can be very fierce, and when the wind was strong the waves were huge and thundered on to the beach, making the *Barbara Mary* rock wildly and tug at her mooring. Godfrey and I would go down to the beach and watch the sea; the air was so filled with spray that you could taste the salt. Godfrey enjoyed sailing, he'd liked it since he sailed with his father at Beaulieu years and years ago. But I had the idea that he was quite glad when it was too rough for us to take the boat out that day.

When the storms died down, off we went in the boat up river to Truro. The sun shone, and the fields and woods looked peaceful, but the water had a powerful swell and the boat heaved. I hadn't been on board for half an hour before I began to feel very sick. I was given to sea-sickness, car-sickness, everything-sickness, and I had sensibly packed anti-seasick tablets in my suitcase. I knew that they worked, although they made me feel drowsy. Determined not to lose face with the Captain, whether I was cabin boy or mate, I secretly took two of the tablets before we set off. No good. The motion of the boat was relentless. I had to creep down to the kitchen (which Godfrey said I must call the galley), to be sick in decent privacy. On almost every trip we took, whether up river or across the bay, although I enjoyed it, I was sick. I was pleased with myself for hiding this. It was quite a coup to be sick and then manage to get back on deck looking unconcerned. One night at home, after a glass of champagne at dinner, I suddenly confessed.

"I want to tell you something," I blurted out. "I know you haven't noticed, and I didn't mean to let you know. But it does seem rather stupid to go on pretending. I keep getting seasick, and creeping down to the kitch – sorry – galley, to be sick."

Godfrey looked astounded. Then began to laugh. I was rather offended. Being sick wasn't as funny as all that. Then, still laughing, he told me that *he* was seasick too. He'd been taking the same tablets. I had bought mine in London, he had gone to Truro for his. When I wasn't in the galley – he had always presumed I was making coffee or cutting the sandwiches – he had taken the chance to go down and be sick too. Both of us, it seemed, had been determined not to disgrace ourselves.

Our twin misfortunes made no difference to our many trips up river to Truro. In rain or shine we set off in the morning, looking like two people in a sepia photograph of Cornish fishermen in the 1900s. Shiny oilskins. Sou'westers. More than one pair of thick socks. And boots which seemed to me to weigh a ton. There our resemblance to the old salts of the past ended, for Godfrey took picnics sometimes which had been sent all the way down from London by Fortnum & Mason's.

He owned a very heavy old-fashioned picnic basket which was not a basket at all: it was in beige-coloured leather and fitted with china, knives and forks and glasses. It even had a section for tools, screwdrivers and spanners; I never worked out why these were necessary on a picnic. He had looked after that picnic basket with care for years, it was a trophy left over from the rich years of the past. I still have the cocktail shaker which belonged in the basket; it was for one person – most unlike Godfrey's character, that. When the hamper arrived from Fortnum's we used to undo it and fill up the basket with tins of caviar *and* smoked salmon; and something I'd never seen before and which Godfrey had ordered for me, splits (i.e. quarter bottles) of champagne.

Godfrey had a talent for treats. He taught me to enjoy things and celebrate things. One day it was goodies from Fortnum's and the next it was bacon sandwiches cooked in our own galley. And both were equally enjoyable.

We always took a change of clothes with us on our expeditions. We sailed up to Truro, moored the *Barbara Mary* and then went into the cabin to change out of our sailing gear into evening dress. We must have looked surprising as we rowed in the dinghy into Truro harbour. Godfrey always took me to dine at the best hotel. We started with cocktails in the bar, and then there was dinner with a good wine. The evening was festive. I remember with shame that although I said I was trying to curb my hefty appetite I used to eat pudding and savoury.

Late in the evening we rowed back to the boat, changed and sailed home down the river in the dark, sometimes by moonlight but often without a star. Usually in silence.

Often, though, we talked a good deal on that holiday. We had long conversations which we both enjoyed, and Godfrey spoke about the theatre and about his life. But we could sail or sit together for an hour without saying a word, and still be content. That's something people often say they can do, but which is actually rare. An hour's silence between two people usually ends by one or other going off into the garden, or to the pub, or to the kitchen, or to the next room to switch on the T.V.

It was an adventure being in Cornwall with Godfrey. The weather was often dreadful but I never cared how heavily it rained, I liked getting my hair dripping wet. I've always loved extremes, it is the normal and the everyday in life which bothers me. I'm good at crises and dramas, no good at all when things are level. That is when boredom sets in. My boredom is an active thing then. Godfrey was easily bored too, and we agreed that it surprised us when people smugly declared "I'm never bored". We thought being bored was a sign that you were bored with yourself. If you never were, you must be complacent.

When we were bored, we read. Godfrey liked new books and the classics, and big parcels arrived from Harrods. But he enjoyed his books about sailing the best.

I had thought, when he first suggested that I might come to stay in Cornwall, that we'd go for blazing country walks. But his bad leg prevented that, and what we did was to saunter. We strolled down gorsy paths or across the fields from which you could see the bay and the slow lines of the waves. We sat on a stile and he rolled one of his cigarettes. Wandering slowly home one afternoon, he taught me a trick he used, something when speaking to help the agility of the tongue. I had to repeat: "Red leather, yellow leather, red leather, yellow leather" over and over again. To start with it seemed impossibly difficult. Godfrey did it so easily and so fast. But I finally learned how to do it as he did – I still use those phrases today. Sometimes we rowed out in the dinghy to the boat, and sat on deck. That was a time for talk, and so was dinner at home.

He began to tell me about the past. I was deeply in

love with the theatre, ignorant and longing to learn. Here was the real thing, a great actor who had begun when he was eight years old. Here was a man who had played at a time which seemed as unreal to me as the days of Kean.

Both his parents were actors, and Godfrey had dual nationality through his American mother. He was born in New York. The Conways, Godfrey said, were a famous American theatre family and his mother had been Marianne Conway. His father, Osmond Tearle, was an actor-manager with his own company in the English provinces. Apart from appearing in America, the provinces were where Osmond intended to stay. He was a superb actor loved by audiences, and convinced that London was of no interest whatsoever. For him the centre of the world was Carlisle. He refused important offers to act in London, chances which would have made him famous. But a London engagement would mean leaving his own work and his own company, even if only for a few months, and that was out of the question.

Beerbohm Tree opened Her Majesty's Theatre in 1897; people called it the best theatre in Europe and even Shaw had to admit that it was "quite the handsomest theatre in London". Tree wrote to Osmond Tearle. Would he play Iago opposite Tree himself as the Moor? It was a remarkable offer, when one remembered that Tearle had never played in London; it showed how big his reputation was among the professionals. Osmond turned Tree down. He wrote and thanked Tree with great politeness, saying how much he appreciated the honour and so on. But he was afraid it was not possible, as he would be leading his own company. In Jarrow.

Tree never forgot or forgave that, and years later he made Godfrey suffer for it.

When Godfrey was only six, something happened

which he remembered for the rest of his life. The family were playing at Leeds, and one evening his father took him on the tram to the theatre. It says a lot about the Tearles' way of life that the small boy was being taken to the theatre at night, instead of being put to bed. There was a tall, spare, distinguished-looking man on the tram whom Godfrey's father knew. They talked together during the journey. The man's face lit up as he smiled at the boy and put his hand on his head.

When Osmond and his son had gone into the theatre, Osmond said solemnly to the child,

"Always remember tonight. It is your first meeting with greatness. That was Henry Irving."

The Tearle family continued to travel . . . all Godfrey's memories of childhood were set in provincial cities. It was in Burnley, when Osmond was playing Richard III, that one of the two children playing the princes in the Tower fell ill. Osmond found himself without a little Duke of York. He sent for his son. Godfrey, by then, was eight-and-a-half-years-old. His father coolly told him that he would not be going to school today.

"You have to rehearse instead."

With the uncanny memory of children, Godfrey already knew the Duke of York's part. He had watched the play night after night and was word perfect. His father rehearsed him all that day, and in the evening Godfrey appeared for the first time on a stage. He had become a working actor.

His mother was alive then, and all the family were actors. Week after week they toured and played. Sundays went by in dirty slow trains, travelling from one city to the next. Godfrey's childhood was spent backstage sitting on skips in dusty theatres, or living in shabby lodgings which changed from week to week. Acting was the only existence the family knew.

Osmond's great grandfather had been a Covent Garden Hamlet, and he himself spent his entire life acting, great roles, melodramas, and always returning to Shakespeare.

Godfrey was awed by his father, and when he talked about Osmond it was of the actor, never of him as a parent. It was his mother whom Godfrey had deeply loved.

We compared our growing up. I thought that mine seemed boring and unexciting when set against his. I had been sent to a number of middle-class girls' schools, and I spent my time (when not being nearly expelled) in learning such middle-class things as schoolgirl French, riding and history of art. I was a fiend in the laboratory, learning to make smells, and was good at games. I also studied the ballet, not only because I enjoyed it but because it got me out of classes in Latin and maths. Being at boarding school and being a child actor did have certain similarities. Both Godfrey and I had been cut off from the rest of the world, for school – like the theatre – is a universe of its own with its own laws and language.

My long-suffering mother, when I finally *did* get expelled, took me home at the age of fourteen and gave up trying to find another school. By the time I was fifteen I was at R.A.D.A., which was much, much too young. I felt that I caught up slightly with Godfrey's career by beginning my own earlier than I should have done.

There was something else that we had in common. We were both only children and I think that can make you lonely by nature. Only children are too passionate and violent in their affections, and I suppose, knowing that, they become cautious. Godfrey never confided easily, and nor did I.

I was very curious about Osmond Tearle, remembering the portrait I had seen of him in the picture gallery at Stratford. I asked Godfrey about him. Osmond had been handsome, and devoted to – obsessed by – work. He loved his wife Marianne deeply, and Godfrey said that when she died "he spent the rest of his life in mourning". The bottle, it seemed, was a comfort to him but although he drank too much it never interfered with his work. As for Osmond and his son, they never connected, were never able to talk to each other. Godfrey simply did not know why. Was it that the young boy was separated from his father by an old-fashioned thing called veneration? It was the father's fault that they were never close, and even when I knew Godfrey he still deeply regretted that there had been no warmth and fun between himself and his father. Osmond remained distant; the gifted actor absorbed by his work. "Just before he died," Godfrey said, "he gave me his gold watch." But I never saw that watch, and I have often wondered what happened to it. Godfrey always wore the watch given him by Owen Nares. Then Godfrey said a sad thing. He never remembered his father ever kissing him.

Everything in the Tearle family was to do with acting, it was matter-of-fact, inescapable, taken for granted. "You just went on and did it," Godfrey said. You knew fifty or sixty parts by heart, you played in Shakespeare or in rubbish, you compensated for the cheap costumes and harsh lighting by talent and determination. You *forced* the audience to accept you in a shabby red velvet cloak as a king. Godfrey had a half-brother, Conway Tearle, who left the provincial touring life and went to America. He became a leading movie actor in the silent days, and then managed the step which ruined so many actors' careers when the talking pictures arrived. He succeeded in transferring from silent to talking films. Conway made the 1929 *Gold Diggers of Broadway*, and in 1936 he starred in Mae West's film *Klondyke Annie*.

What I wanted to hear most, and what Godfrey enjoyed telling me, was about his own life in those far-off days. I listened, rapt, to stories of the Edwardian theatre. Godfrey loved to talk and I was the world's most attentive audience, glad to listen to him for hours. I didn't know a thing about the theatre of the past and I didn't have to. I didn't understand much of what he talked about, but imagination filled the spaces of my total ignorance. Besides, I never minded making a fool of myself.

"Lewis Waller played the lead," Godfrey might say.

"Lewis who?"

He always laughed, looking quite pleased when I said that I didn't know who he was talking about.

It was not all harmony on our first holiday together. Both of us were moody. I think it had been quite a long time since he had had a companion with him all the time. The last few years had been freedom for Godfrey, the time to sow his final wild oats. Suddenly, here I was in his life. He used to get broody, as all creative people do, grow quiet, glower or stare into space. Looking across the room or the deck at him and seeing that expression, I used to decide it was his Cornish/Jewish/American blood which made him moody. Some mixture. He might play the English gentleman onstage, he had done so for years and he had that thrilling English voice, but I never thought he was particularly English. He could be so charming when he wanted to be. He certainly wasn't equable.

It was quite difficult for me in a way. I had to be careful how I walked. Sometimes I could get away with being cheeky and he looked amused, but sometimes I knew it would be wise to shut up. My instincts have always been quite good. I try to follow the advice in Ecclesiastes, to remember that "To everything there is a season . . . time to embrace, and a time to refrain from embracing . . . a time to keep silent, and a time to speak." I didn't intrude. Looking back, I think perhaps I was too careful, because sometimes it is quite good to be intrusive. People hold up their hands to fend you off, but aren't they occasionally glad when you ignore that and run towards them?

I am not sure what made Godfrey sombre at those times. The actor's life, I suppose. It never basically changes, and however famous you become you have to face rejections and failures. Looking at me, he'd suddenly use a phrase he had picked up from me.

"I'm in one of my Celtic glooms." And he would add,

"Let's have a moan. You start. Or shall I?"

The mood changed as the weather did, and we went off sailing again. He was happy on the sea and I like water too. I was born in a monsoon, and storms make me feel wonderful. Next to storms, I enjoy rough seas; when I'm not being sick, that is. We loved the wild weather, the pelting rain and sudden hot October sun. One calmish day, with a good deal of preparation, Godfrey decided that we would sail across the Channel to Le Havre.

We were both in high spirits. The sea was flatter than usual, the *Barbara Mary* swooped along, and I knew my role as first mate well by now. We were soon on deck, drinking a glass of champagne – in Godfrey's case a martini – and enjoying some baked beans on toast. But Godfrey must have got his directions utterly mixed. I don't know if he read the compass or charts wrongly or misjudged the way the wind was blowing. In any case, after a good long sail and a lot of fun, we saw the coastline, sailed closer – and found ourselves approaching Plymouth Sound. There are not many captains who set off from Cornwall for France and sail with a flourish to Plymouth, not thirty miles up the coast.

But he liked to sail. It amused and interested him,

and he liked its lore and its vocabulary. I still have a shelf filled with his books, all of which are crammed with information about riding lights and splicing knots and what to do when the boat drags her anchor.

Although the sea was often rough, the water was warm after the long hot summer, and we were both strong swimmers. We went to the beach almost every day to swim. Godfrey never fussed about me when we swam and the breakers came rolling in. He never shouted "Don't go out so deep!" Just as, all the time I knew him, he never once asked me if I was cold. He knew I could dive through the waves, and he knew I wouldn't sit shivering when I could perfectly well go upstairs and get a jacket.

There was a closeness between us. I can't give it a name, I can only say that there was no hesitating and no battle of the sexes. He wasn't looking for a daughter – or was he? He had never had children and had always declared to me that he considered actors shouldn't; life in the theatre was too uncertain and too difficult. I suppose he thought that because his own childhood had not been happy and his own father was not a father but an actor. We *were* happy, though. Once during the Cornish holiday somebody innocently spoke to Godfrey and called me his granddaughter and Godfrey said, "No, she's my great granddaughter."

He wasn't always indulgent to me. He liked to give me treats, but he never let me get away with anything. Yet there was another side to that, and in a way I was looked after. One morning when we came down the beach path to the shore before setting off in the dinghy, there were some French letters lying on the sand. It was such a secluded beach it was just the place two people would choose. I saw Godfrey hastily trying to get rid of the things before I had noticed them. I was amused and rather pleased because he thought I needed protecting in that way. He was protecting himself, too. He didn't like that sort of carelessness – it offended his sense of decency.

In the evenings, not only when we went to Truro in the boat, we always changed for dinner. My puppy fat was beginning to go; it must have been all the healthy exercise as cabin boy sluicing down the deck. When I was dressed for the evening I looked quite nice. I had a chiffon dress he liked which was navy blue, both sexy and schoolgirlish. The colour which Godfrey detested for evenings was brown, and for years I never wore brown at night . . .

As for Godfrey, he looked wonderful. He had a good figure and a graceful way of moving. He always looked well turned out. It was not the age of the duffle coat and jeans, and if it had been he would have disliked them both. Even on the boat when we were dressed for work he looked good. He had long-fingered aristocratic hands, the best I have ever seen. I remember how startled I was in London when he had them manicured. He was the first man I had known to do such a thing.

So there we were in the drawing-room of his Cornish house, looking chic and – to present-day eyes – got up to the nines. He stood by the fireplace drinking a dry martini; cocktails were his favourite. He ate and drank sparingly, and his favourite food was Haddock Monte Carlo. Thinking about the holiday, I do remember quite a lot of champagne which Godfrey ordered for me. But I had often drunk it with my mother to celebrate a success or get us through a disaster so that treat wasn't a complete surprise.

One cold morning Godfrey and I got up at the crack of dawn; he had arranged for us to go out with some local fishermen. We were with them in the trawler before five in the morning. They trawled with huge nets, and we saw the nets get heavy and the whole wriggling silver load pulled in, herring or mackerel, I can't remember which. Godfrey and I were muffled in our oiled woollen sweaters and oilskins and socks and seaboots, and we drank coffee laced with whisky, which was handed round to everybody to keep out the cold. The fishermen treated him as one of themselves; that's a gift the best actors have, they can become like the people they are with, take on the skin of someone else even if it is only for an hour.

We were invited out to meet the other kind of local people, those who lived in posh houses. They were charming and friendly and – as the fishermen had done – treated Godfrey as one of themselves. He was in his role of sailor and distinguished local resident, but not actor. We never stayed long, though.

The holiday was like the weather, it was a mixture of good and bad, of fun and silence, of expansive moods and Celtic gloom. An experienced and glamorous actor, and a girl whose acting life hadn't even begun.

Sometimes in the evening we drove into Truro to go to the cinema. We both liked films, and had got into the habit at Stratford where we often saw practically half the company also sitting in the two and sixes. At Stratford, Godfrey took me to see Laurence Olivier's *Hamlet*, which he enormously admired. Unlike many actors who remain – extraordinary as it seems – still jealous when they have become world famous, Godfrey was delighted when an actor pulled off a great success. He used to say, ''There's always room at the top.''

Even in Cornwall and on holiday he was busy. Letters came for him in shoals from all over the world. That was something which happened to a famous man even then. Of course, like everything else connected with the arts, it has grown much larger now that people in the news are universally known. Actors or pop stars or footballers or best-selling novelists need to hire people to cope with their gigantic post-bags these days. Somebody told me that when John le Carré wrote his first big success, *The Spy Who Came in From the Cold*, he described success as similar to being in a car accident. It was not as bad as that for Godfrey, but his mail was still exhaustingly large. Apart from letters about business and a big fan mail, he always had plans going for new work, things on and off the boil. There were directors trying to persuade him to play roles that didn't interest him, and Godfrey wanting roles which – like Macbeth – would need a great deal of time, money and luck to set up.

Quite suddenly the holiday came to an end. I was telephoned by the B.B.C. in Birmingham. They offered me a part in a radio play. I would play the daughter in a family drama. It was going to be quite a production.

Godfrey didn't even say he was sorry that I had to leave Cornwall. There was no question of my *not* going, we both knew that. This was my job as it was his, and we were aware that I needed all the experience that I could get.

He drove me to Truro and put me on the train. Our parting wasn't depressing, it was a beginning. This was how our life was going to be from now on.

As the train left the station and began to hurry east through Cornish valleys, and there were sudden flashes of sea, my thoughts were on Godfrey. Cornwall was like him. It was rugged and strong, simple and self-reliant. Dangerous, too. Stratford had never seemed to be his place except when he was actually onstage. It had been, for him, too provincial.

Five

I went to Birmingham, and we telephoned each other every day. It was to be a big broadcast, and in those days a radio play took four or five days to rehearse and went out live. I enjoyed it all and have been in love with radio ever since.

When I came back to London, Godfrey was at Paddington waiting to meet my train, wearing wonderful pale tweed plus fours. I never asked him to meet me and he had never said that he would. But there he was. He didn't tell me whether he had wanted to stay on in Cornwall or whether he had come back to London because of me.

We hadn't discussed where I was going to live. Godfrey had a flat in Queen Anne Street, off Harley Street, and my parents still lived in Westbourne Terrace. Before I went to Stratford I lived in a bed-sit in the Cromwell Road, but I still kept most of my clothes and all my books at my parents' flat. Now, as it turned out, I lived in my parents' flat *and* with Godfrey, sometimes in one place and sometimes in the other. The arrangement suited us. My parents accepted Godfrey for what he was, a man of their own generation but unique. I'm sure they believed that – rebellious by nature as I was – if they tried to stop me making what they must have thought was a mistake, I'd go on to make a worse one. They were clever and wise and kind. And very, very unconventional for that time.

Godfrey was always working, but I was hardly working at all. I went to audition after audition, being offered nothing. I'd already begun to recognise that rejection is the name of the game. An actor must try to be detached about not getting work; must find a way of being amused at his or her own attempts and failures. For the actor is a commodity, often not judged for talent, but for a dozen other reasons, from physical appearance to the director's taste. Often, too, a part is got by default. Somebody else is unobtainable and by chance the director suddenly decides, "Yes, you'll do." It's true that an actor needs talent; but timing and luck as well.

When I was not fretting over my lack of a career, Godfrey and I did have a marvellous time. "Let's use the town," was a phrase of his, and that was what we did. We went out to meals or galleries, to movies or the opera. We went to the theatre constantly. His flat was large, in an old-fashioned mansion building. The rooms were spacious and lofty, there were two bathrooms and an impressively vast drawing-room. A married couple cooked for him and generally looked after him, just as in Cornwall. But there, as far as I was concerned, the resemblance ended. The Cornish couple had been country people and very kind, making me feel welcome. The London couple bitterly disapproved and showed it whenever Godfrey was not actually present. The man was an ex-colonial who had been in the regular army, possibly the Indian army. He said he had been a major but I always thought him slightly dubious. Perhaps he felt he had come down in the world . . . I don't know. But he was much too fond of Godfrey, too possessive and devoted. He was jealous of the girl who had now made her appearance, who was young and carefree and in his book an immoral nobody. But Godfrey was easy and kind, I'm sure he didn't see all this. I wasn't going to tell him that when his back was turned I was treated with such cruel dislike.

During the winter of 1949 Godfrey had to go to Spain to make a film, *Decameron Nights*. He always said that he was no good in films, and in this case he added that he had decided to do the film only because of the money. It was typical of him that he thoroughly enjoyed it, and made a friend of Louis Jourdan who played the romantic lead. Before leaving for Spain, Godfrey made a drawing of my foot; he said he would try and buy me some Spanish shoes. He and Louis Jourdan found a Spanish shoemaker who made me some delicate handmade shoes, high-heeled, classic, and fitting miraculously.

While Godfrey was in Spain I missed him very much. I missed his companionship, his love, and his critical eye. He had said that I must treat Queen Anne Street as my home, but I kept well away from the ex-major until Godfrey came back. In the meantime I was busy toiling about trying to get work; it did begin to come sporadically, mostly on the radio.

If life with Godfrey in Cornwall had alternated between bacon sandwiches and caviar, the differences when he returned to London were even more marked. On one day I would be snatching a hasty coffee and a cheese sandwich with other out-of-work actors between auditions, and then the same evening I would be at the Savoy Grill with Godfrey. It meant dressing up. Girls going out for dinner then used to look as if they were on their way to the court of the Empress Eugènie – we were bare-shouldered, our dresses boned and with enormous bouffant skirts. I had an expensive dress, my favourite, which Godfrey had bought for me. It was grey lace with an underskirt of pink, and I used to have a struggle to get into its boned top and to do up the tight waist. When we bought it I had lied about my size.

Soon after returning from Spain, Godfrey was asked if he would take over Ralph Richardson's part in *The Heiress* at the Haymarket Theatre. The play, from the book by Henry James, *Washington Square*, had been running for some time, with Richardson as the father to Peggy Ashcroft's doomed and eventually icily revengeful daughter. It was an enormous success. Wendy Hiller was now taking over from Peggy Ashcroft, and Godfrey agreed to take over from Ralph Richardson. Years before, Godfrey had done the same thing – taken over the Richardson part that time in *The Amazing Doctor Clitterhouse*. Godfrey never minded taking over another actor's part. He was unworried by comparisons. Often his performances were very different, sometimes he was better than his predecessor. The critics always said that he brought some quality of his own to whatever part he took over.

"Will you hear me my lines, Jill?"

Settled again for a few days in Queen Anne Street, I sat on the arm of the sofa with the script in my hand. I was to read the Ashcroft/Hiller role. I decided to do it well, and wondered what it would be like actually to play it. (Years later I did it on television, and it was as difficult, and as satisfying, as I'd imagined.)

Godfrey, meanwhile, went to fetch his shoes. Not one pair but half a dozen which he then lined up on the table. He added the shoe polish, black and brown, and some brushes. He always cleaned his shoes when he was learning his lines, it helped his concentration. Speaking aloud, deeply absorbed, Godfrey made his shoes shine to a blinding brightness. When he had finished them, off he went in search of mine. They were polished with masculine vigour too. I've never had such clean shoes in my life since then. Anybody who happened to call at the flat while Godfrey was learning his lines had their shoes seized. One afternoon my mother arrived to see us. She was immediately requested to take off her shoes. Soon they were glittering, as Godfrey went through one of his long *Heiress* speeches.

It was difficult for me to see him as the great actor

any more. There he was, repeating the rolling cadences of Jamesian lines in that extraordinary voice while he wielded a boot brush and a tin of Cherry Blossom polish.

When I went with him to the Haymarket Theatre before the opening, I noticed he had the Number Two dressing-room, which was upstairs. It was Godfrey's rule to give his leading actress the star dressing-room, just as he always gave her the top billing. His gallantry bothered me; the dressing-room which he had was up a flight of stairs, and that was bad for his leg.

During the run of *The Heiress* in which he was superb, Godfrey became ill. His doctor said that he must stay in bed for two or three weeks, and his understudy took over. Godfrey was an appalling patient – "patient" was just what he was not. He was difficult and irritable, he refused to make the best of things. It was a nightmare. I didn't buzz round him because I knew he would dislike it, and I didn't behave as if I were a nurse. I just tried to be useful and to keep him amused. He had a good doctor, and Sir Horace Evans, the heart specialist, came to see him.

Godfrey was dismissive to me about his illness. It was nothing, he said, nothing at all. It would be over in a flash. Propped up in bed, he said he wouldn't talk about his boring illness. He was making plans again to put on another production of *Macbeth*.

Then, to my utter relief, he was better and back at the theatre, and we began to "use the town". Thinking about his flat, I realise now what few possessions he had. He told me, when he talked about his first marriage, that there had been a time when it had been the reverse. Houses, a Rolls, a chauffeur, servants, chow dogs, charity performances, golf with people as famous as himself. He'd liked it all. Sables and diamonds for Mary Malone, his first wife. But by the time I knew Godfrey he had said goodbye to the posses-

sion-weighted past. I believe that in the heart of every
actor you'll find a gypsy. Like the gypsy, he has the
trick of moving on; like Toad in *The Wind in the Willows*
the actor's imagination is caught by what's next. He is
here today and in the middle of next week tomorrow.
Many successful actors get loaded down with possessions. They buy big houses and horses and Georgian
silver and Picassos. But they are playing a part; actors
should not have roots, they should not be immovable,
and the loss of such things should never be allowed to
damage their talent. They should always manage to
move on. Godfrey had had the rich time and it was
now behind him. There were no paintings on the walls
of that bachelorish flat, except one or two water-
colours of boats and seascapes by Cornish artists.
There was a photograph of the *Barbara Mary*. He had a
silver watch from Owen Nares. A nice blue jar for his
tobacco. Not one single thing that had belonged to his
father.

Godfrey was the most generous man I have ever
met. He liked giving. He gave me all kinds of things:
records and books and clothes and flowers. To celebrate the first year we had known each other, he took
me to the Burlington Arcade and bought me a great
aquamarine ring – aquamarines were his favourite
stones. He told me kindly that I had beautiful feet, and
as by now I had worn the Spanish shoes until they
were falling to pieces, he took me to Rayne's in Bond
Street. I tried on some narrow, high-heeled, strappy
navy blue shoes which were very fetching, and
walked up and down the salon while Godfrey studied
my feet. Then he said to the girl who was serving us,

"What other colours have you in the same style?"

"Black, and beige."

"We'll have all three."

I'm good at being given things, but as I've said
earlier, Godfrey was hopeless at it. It was a fault that

he so disliked accepting presents. I was in Captain Watts' sailing shop, buying him boat knife after boat knife. He always looked quite pleased to have them, but he had a drawer full of them by now. So when I passed a bookshop I always went in to ask if they had a section on Sailing. I was trying to find him a new book on tying knots.

During the run of *The Heiress*, Godfrey made another film, *White Corridors*, in which he starred with Googie Withers, Moira Lister and James Donald. Godfrey played a surgeon and gave a very hammy performance, lifting up those graceful hands of his and waiting for obsequious nurses to pull on his rubber gloves. He remained convinced that he was a bad film actor. But I liked him in *White Corridors*. I thought the surgeon had something of the arrogance of his Othello.

I got my first real theatre job that winter at the Westminster Theatre in a production of *Pickwick Papers*, a straight adaptation of the book, with no music. I was playing a servant again – Sam Weller's girl friend. My previous line of parts, from young boy to whore plus all those waiting women at Stratford, hadn't been exactly taxing. I wasn't any good at the Dickensian maidservant either. But I didn't know that someone in films had come to a performance, and told John Huston about me.

Godfrey was at the Haymarket and I was at the Westminster, and we used to arrive home late, and have supper by the fire. But *Pickwick* didn't run for long and soon I was looking for work again. Godfrey was sympathetic, but didn't offer to help. He never said to any of the directors whom he knew, "There's this young actress, Jill Bennett, who . . ." In a way I believe he felt being with him was a hindrance to me. There I was in the Caprice having lunch with him, often meeting his famous and hard-working friends.

What I did not have was what I desperately needed to get without influence, off my own bat. A job.

Godfrey and I had met most of each other's friends by now. It was part of his generosity that he was kind and hospitable to mine. His friends were judges, generals and doctors, and a good many American and English actors. Sebastian Shaw came to Queen Anne Street and so did John Gielgud, who had quite forgotten me in *Much Ado*, carrying those artificial lilies. I'm sure he thought he had never seen me before. Godfrey's friends were very nice to me, but I must have been a surprise. I didn't look a bit like a mistress. I didn't have a mink coat or a single diamond. I looked, as Godfrey had witheringly remarked once, as if I ought to come on with a hockey stick. Actually I was bad at hockey and good at lacrosse. He got that wrong.

So my career had ground to a halt again. I went to auditions because I knew I mustn't stop looking for work, ever. But I hadn't a glimmer of hope that I would be chosen for any part. I've sometimes thought I must have been a disappointment to Godfrey at that time. Although I was young I was not carefree. If I had been he would never have sent me all those telegrams wishing me happiness. There's a great jolly song in Disney's *Pinocchio* which makes me grimace. "An actor's life is fun." Yes, it is. It's also disjointed and uncertain, and the task is relentless. You are your own instrument and all that you have is yourself.

Godfrey knew I wasn't light-hearted although I larked about. Perhaps if I had been, he would never have asked me to walk on the airfield with him. When John Gielgud cast me as Amanda in *Private Lives* years later, he said, with a certain flourish, "You're like Amanda. Doomed to tragedy." I suppose it is better than a quiet life in Penge.

Then, while Godfrey was filming *White Corridors* by day and playing *The Heiress* every night at the Haymarket, I went to the St. James's Theatre for a reading. Laurence Olivier was putting on a new play by Denis Cannan, *Captain Carvallo*. Olivier had apparently seen me at Stratford which was why I had been sent for. I was astonished, remembering my Bianca. I thought – among the hundreds of girls he has seen in the last year he actually noticed me. The play was sent to me through the post in advance and I saw with a sigh that the part was for a maid. Another maid. A sulky rebellious kind of girl this time.

I arrived at the St. James's Theatre in a state of shaking nerves and totally without hope: reading for Olivier was more than flesh and blood could stand. I kept telling myself that this was a *real* waste of time. When my turn came, being slightly dyslectic, I read very badly, the pages of the script positively rattling in my trembling hands.

Olivier gave me the part. When I heard, I practically fainted.

He himself was directing *Captain Carvallo*, and to a beginner he was both wonderful and maddening to work with. At the start of the play I had to sweep the floor. After I had done this two or three times, Olivier jumped up from his seat in the stalls and came up onstage. He took the broom from me.

"Try it like this," he said, and began to sweep.

He made even sweeping a floor sexy and funny.

The play, a Ruritanian romance previously seen in Bristol, starred Godfrey's Desdemona, the stately devotee of fireworks, Diana Wynyard. She was still very leading-ladyish with me and did not bother to hide that she thought I was no good. She herself *was* good. She had a strong stage presence, she could be both moving and comic, and her voice had an edge which was very useful in performance. It was a most upper-class voice, but that was how actors spoke in the 1950s. Everybody in a play, except peasants or servants,

GODFREY SEYMOUR TEARLE

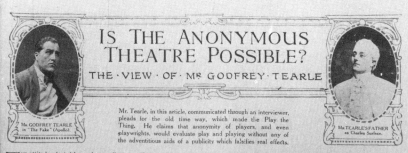

IS THE ANONYMOUS THEATRE POSSIBLE?

THE · VIEW · OF · Mᴿ GODFREY · TEARLE

Mr. Tearle, in this article, communicated through an interviewer, pleads for the old time way, which made the Play the Thing. He claims that anonymity of players, and even playwrights, would evaluate play and playing without any of the adventitious aids of a publicity which falsifies real effects.

Mr GODFREY TEARLE in "The Fake" (Apollo).

Mr TEARLE'S FATHER as Charles Surface.

THE attitude adopted by modern audiences towards stage players is stifling to the versatility of actors and actresses. Playgoers of to-day want to see men and women who are leaders o' the theatrical profession in the type of part they have decided is best for their own enjoyment. They deliberately attach their own limitations to the work of their most popular stars. Not for one instant do they pause to consider the effect of this attitude of mind or Dramatic Art as a whole, or the individual art of each player, in particular.

As I see it, things grow worse in this respect, not better. Players of to-day are expected to do more acting off the stage than in the playhouse. Old-time players spent more hours daily inside the four walls of their office—the theatre—than many of our young actors and actresses spend in a week. This, perhaps, is not altogether their fault; it is largely due to the "lionising" of individuals thrust into the public eye through their chosen profession.

Present-day insistence on, and familiarity with, the personal side and private lives of the Servants of the Drama does not make for better Art; nor does it induce versatility or inspire ambition. The advent of the commercial manager, the Press agent, the photographer, gossip columns in the daily papers, the linking of Stage and Society—all these factors, to my mind, tend to strangle the art of the actor.

Harvey, Leslie Henson, Cyril Maude, Fay Compton, Gladys Cooper, Hilda Trevelyan in rôles they—the audience—choose to label "a du Maurier part," and so on. This is cramping, in itself. In justice to the paying public whose money keeps the theatre alive, I do not deny that playgoers of to-day, as a whole, are more deeply concerned with Dramatic Art than at any other period in the history of the playhouse. But the trouble is that their concern follows the wrong line of thought, and serves to stultify and choke the work of professional players who strive in all sincerity to entertain them, while upholding the highest ideals of the drama.

I THINK the present playgoing public asks less in *quantity*, but far more in *quality* than their ancestors. Everything behind the footlights

YET once a similar display of versatility was not only accepted, but *expected* from all players of any real standing. We could get back to it, I am positive, if the Anonymous Theatre became an actual fact. Men and women would cease to matter, personally. They would become the puppets all good players should be, in the best sense of that word. If their acting did not reach a sufficiently high level the theatre would cease to provide them with an income. *Once names ceased to count only good acting would be tolerated.*

IF actors' names were not made public, playgoers would patronise the drama not to watch one individual artist, but to witness a certain type of play, confident that it would be well played. Theatres would choose their particular type of entertainment, and stick to it; audiences that their special star. Unless the level or performances proved high, in such conditions, a theatre would find itself doing no business at all, if deprived of the bolstering conveniently provided nowadays by star names, in electric-light-letters. Salaries would soon find their true mark, productions would cease to be exaggeratedly expensive; general improvement .... land should result.

Top left: *Osmond Tearle, Godfrey's father, was Charles Surface in* The School for Scandal. *Osmond was a superb actor, led his own provincial company, and refused many rich offers to appear in London.*

Bottom left: *Godfrey at eight and a half, just at the time his father sent for him to play the Duke of York (one of the little princes in the Tower) in* Richard III. *This photograph was probably taken for publicity.*

Above: *Godfrey came from three generations of actors, on both sides of the family. His American mother was one of a famous family, the Conways, who were given star billing when they toured England.*

99

Right: *This bi-plane is quite a surprise; I was never told about it. But Godfrey was inventive, though I'm not sure this invention was particularly good . . .*
Below: *Godfrey in 1907 as Silvius in* As You Like It. *Oscar Asche gave him his first chance at His Majesty's. Godfrey's good looks were noticed by critics and audiences: he was "un jeune homme beau". He never thought himself in the least handsome.*

FLIGHT

aspect-ratios. As this affects the pressure distribution, it would affect the lifting power and also the centre of pressure, so that experimental determinations made with square surfaces could not be safely applied to the design of the surfaces more commonly used.

The above suggests the reason for the downward curvature at the outer ends of the Wright and (I believe) the latest Blériot machines.

It also suggests the possible increase of automatic stability by variations in the plan-form, in conjunction with proper profile curvature, the whole, I think you will agree, offering a most inviting field for investigation.

Dayton, Ohio.   F. C. MOCK.

MR. McNEILL'S BIPLANE.

[884]   I have been very interested to read letter 782, in your excellent paper.

Mr. McNeill and myself have been *thinking in parallels.*

I enclose a rough sketch of my biplane, which may interest you.

Practically the only difference in our machines is that he uses side curtains to prevent escape of air, while I have adopted a system

of curved planes, which I maintain has the same effect, and does away with the danger from side winds.

I fancy, too, that my construction would be stronger than Mr. McNeill's. However, in the face of his letter, I thought the enclosed might interest you.

Portland Place.   GODFREY TEARLE.

ANOTHER BRITISH MACHINE.

[885]   I enclose two photos of a monoplane, which I hope you will consider worthy of illustration in your journal.

This machine was built by my brother and a friend (both engineers) and possesses several novel features. The frame is made of steel tubing, welded by oxy-acetylene process ; the backbone is of bamboo, and the main plane is in one piece, and can easily be

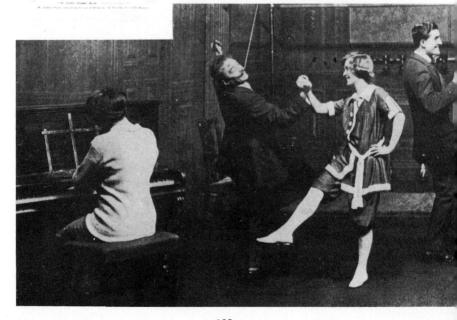

Left and below: *Barrie's enchanting play,* Quality Street, *at the Duke of York's in 1913 gave Godfrey the pleasure of playing opposite Cathleen Nesbitt. He also played Captain Hook in Barrie's* Peter Pan *at matinées.* Bottom: The Amazons *at the Duke of York's in 1912. Godfrey danced and sang – he was at home in musicals and enjoyed appearing in them.*

Edwardians were fascinated by the art of acting – amateur dramatics were all the rage in the big country houses. Godfrey's article (bottom, with detail below) gives a few (to my mind) exaggerated lessons. Right: Another article . Theatregoers collected postcards of the star actors. The postcard (opposite left) shows Godfrey in Faust, in Beerbohm Tree's 1908 production at His Majesty's. Opposite right: His fanmail photograph, with God-

Are Women Frauds ?

By
Godfrey Tearle.

Illustrated by
A. Wallis Mills.

"If women are frauds it is only because they are forced to be—by men," says Mr. Godfrey Tearle in the following spirited defence of the opposite sex. Mr. Tearle enhanced an already great reputation by his magnificent performance as Boris Androvsky in *The Garden of Allah*, and his opinion on this delicate subject will be of intense interest to his countless admirers.—[Ed. R.M.]

SPEAKING for myself, I want a lot of proof before asserting definitely that they are.

It seems a common practice to denounce women—*en masse*—as frauds, a general custom to take it for granted that they are—that they *must* be—without any endeavour to find out if such a belief is justified, or if it holds even a vestige of truth.

If I can believe what I am told, if I am to credit my own ears and eyes in everyday theatrical life, nothing remains but to say, quite candidly, that women *are* frauds, but—

Yes, there is a "but" in this, as in every other case. The "but" I want to advance is this: If women are frauds, it is only because they are forced to be—by men.

For my own sex I hold no brief. For the women we condemn so hastily, so thoughtlessly, one feels a great sympathy and pity. After all, they are principally what men make them. They live, most of them, with one main idea in their minds—to please the opposite sex. And so, if they are frauds, or insincere, or lacking in true affection, is it

The fluffy, foolish female is very often the direct result of the Tired Business Man's craving for relaxation and amusement.

After all, a woman's main business in life is to find out what men like—or what *her* man likes—and cater for it. Having found out, she is obviously a fool if she doesn't! In catering for a man's wishes, or weaknesses, she doubtless fools him, perhaps acts many little lies, or voices many insincerities. But is that really fraud? I am inclined to believe not.

It is principally a question of bluff. Life is one long series of bluffs—between rival

is loved by another man, who writes her a

Fig. 5. *Remorse*. Here attitude also plays an important part in explaining the situation

WOMAN'S WORK

The sphere of woman's work is ever widening, and now there are innumerable professions and businesses by which the enterprising woman can obtain a livelihood. The object of this section of EVERY WOMAN'S ENCYCLOPÆDIA, therefore, is to point out the high-road to success in these careers. Ideas are also given to the stay-at-home girl which should help her to supplement her dress allowance and at the same time amuse herself. The subjects dealt with include :

Professions	Woman's Work in the Colonies	Little Ways of Making Pin-Money
Doctor	Canada	Photography
Civil Servant	Australia	Chicken Rearing
Nurse	South Africa	Sweet Making
Dressmaker	New Zealand	China Painting
Actress	Colonial Nurses	Bee Keeping
Musician	Colonial Teachers	Toy Making
Secretary	Training for Colonies	Ticket Writing,
Governess	Colonial Outfits	etc., etc.
Dancing Mistress, etc.	Farming, etc.	

frey's inevitable cigarette. He used to send off hundreds of these cards every week. Bottom: The Land of Promise by Somerset Maugham (Duke of York's, 1914), an updated version of The Taming of the Shrew, described by W. Macqueen-Pope as "a battle of wits . . . between the male denied his conjugal rights and the female who denies him". It was one of God- frey's "by God, you shall!" parts. The play was a great success, but there was one criticism of his performance: women found it impossible to believe that any girl could resist him.

Godfrey Tearle as "Valentine" in "Faust".

MR GODFREY TEARLE

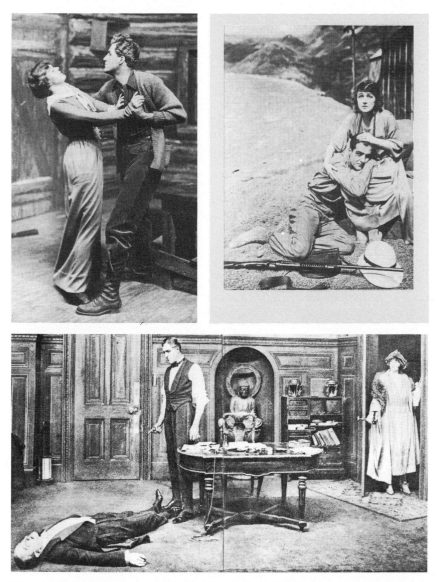

Top left: *"If you don't submit willingly, by God I'll take you as the trappers in the old days used to take the squaws."* The Land of Promise.

Top right: *Godfrey and Madge Titheradge in* The Garden of Allah *at Drury Lane, 1920.*

Above: The Sign on the Door, *at the Playhouse in* September 1921, *was the play in which he starred opposite the glorious Gladys Cooper. He was deeply in love with her then.*

Opposite: The Faithful Heart *at the Comedy in 1921 was described by A. Haddon in* Green Room Gossip *as having "a winning tenderness, a simple humanity and homely humour". Godfrey had to age twenty years in the play, beginning as a young fourth officer in a Union liner, returning as a lieutenant-colonel. It was considered one of the best plays of the season.*

Below: *Matinée idols were also sporting chaps but Godfrey's golfing style was far better than his game.*

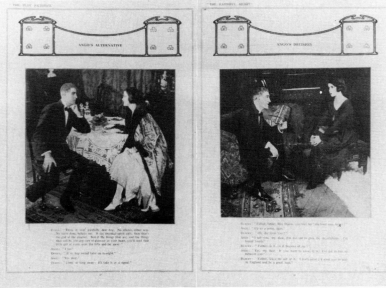

"THE WAY OF AN EAGLE

AT THE ADELPHI

MARJORIE GORDON AND GODFREY TEARLE

A BARRIE REVIVAL

"What Every Woman Knows"
Enthusiastically Received

Did any husbands go home uneasy from the Apollo last night? For "What Every Woman Knows" is all her man's shortcomings, and most especially that whatever good thing he has done, he likes to think that he has done it all by himself.

This comedy of Sir James Barrie is a welcome revival, and will help to explain to the younger generation, who have only seen his later plays, on what his reputation was founded.

He wrote this shrewd, amusing play in the happy days before he had acquired his mother obsession. Here the fun always gets the upper hand, and every time that you are afraid of a lapse he recovers himself with a joke. How refreshing and unusual to see four acts, and none of them weak, and the whole a marvel of construction.

I find it hard to believe that "Maggie" could have ever loved such an intolerably conceited self-centred fellow as "John," and I should have liked him to have a redeeming trait or two. But no one could help loving "Maggie," even if she had no charm. The excitement of the election is well worked to a crescendo, and the management has been lavish with electors who form a perfectly natural crowd.

The play is perfectly cast, and Mr. Holman Clark's production is a delight. Miss Hilda Trevelyan seems not a day older than when she first played the part, and is every bit as delightful. Mr. Godfrey Tearle is excellent, and in his final breakdown acted with the most amazing sincerity. Indeed everyone was excellent, but of course Lady

Opposite: *The kind of romantic poster that made Godfrey's adoring fans queue for hours at the stage door.*

Left: *From a page of Godfrey's 1923 notices, including Barrie's* What Every Woman Knows. *He never* dreamed of keeping his notices, but his wives did. I still have bookfuls of them. Below: *He played the lead in* Arlequin *at the Empire in 1922. He looks wonderfully graceful, but (bottom) seems to be wearing a hairnet.*

THE PROFESSION TAKES A DAY OFF.

MR. GODFREY TEARLE AND MR. OWEN NARES SEEK TO ESCAPE THEIR FLAPPER ADMIRERS.

THE MAGAZINE P...

Proprietors .. .. THE HIPPODROME (GOLDERS GREEN, LTD.)
Managing Director .. .. J. C. CLAVERING
Manager .. .. HUGH BAKER
Assistant Manager .. .. A. P. ALGAR
Musical Director .. .. ÁLBERT H. DUNLOP

EVERY EVENING at 8.0

Matinees : THURSDAY and SATURDAY at 2.30

Preceded by **GODFREY TEARLE**

In Selections from his Shakespearean and other Repertoire

PERSONAL VISIT (under the Management of PERCY BURTON) of

GODFREY TEARLE

AND

MARY MALONE

In a New Modern Play

"THE ACQUITTAL"

By RITA WEIMAN. (By arrangement with GEORGE M. COHAN)

Characters in the order of their appearance :

Barton	EDGAR B. PAYNE
Nellie	KITTY GORDON
Madeleine Winthrop	...MARY MALONE
Stephen Hammond, M.D.	RONALD BAYNE
Ethel Craig	ELEANOR STREET
Philip Conway	GODFREY TEARLE
Kenneth Winthrop	HESKETH PEARSON
Sir Robert Armstrong, K.C. ...	J. LISTER-WILLIAMS
Michael McCarthy	MAURICE GREW
George Ainsley	...LEONARD TROLLOPE
Jane Wilson	CECILY DERRICK

The play produced by GODFREY TEARLE

Top: *Theatre cartoons like these were very popular in magazines, including the Tatler, the Sketch, and Punch.*

Above: *Godfrey with his wife, Mary Malone, and* (left) *a page from the programme of* The Acquittal, *1928.*

Opposite top: *Godfrey's Hamlet was not admired – he looked far too strong and athletic, and he himself quoted to me the notice which said he looked as if he should have been a double-*

BAD NEWS FOR THE KING

Saul . . . . Mr. Godfrey Tearle
Ophir . . . . . . Mr. Leon Quartermaine
Nathan . . . . . Mr. Ion Swinley

blue at Wittenberg.
Above and left: *Barrie again. The Boy David was written especially for Elizabeth Bergner, then at the height of her astonishing fame with the London theatre public. People queued all day to see her performances. The Boy David was starry in every way. Augustus John designed it, and Komisarjevsky directed.*

"THE FLASHING STREAM"

Above: *When Charles Morgan wrote* The Flashing Stream *in 1938, he and Godfrey went into management with the play together. Margaret Rawlings starred with Godfrey, and Godfrey's third wife Barbara Mary played the Rawlings part on tour. The penny (opposite) was a symbol – no money was exchanged between Godfrey and Charles. It is set into a (signed) silver ashtray, which I now have.*
Right: *A still from* One of Our Aircraft is Missing. *The film was directed by*

Michael Powell, who persuaded Godfrey to return to acting.

Top: *Hitchcock's famous* The Thirty-Nine Steps. *Godfrey (left, with Helen Haye as his wife and Robert Donat as Richard Hannay, the hero) plays the arch villain.*

Above: *Critics said that Godfrey's performance as the failed, drunken actor in Emlyn Williams's* The Light of Heart *(Apollo, 1940) was one of his most outstanding for many years. It was while he was playing this role that he decided to retire to Cornwall.*

111

GODFREY TEARLE AS OTHELLO.

Opposite: top and bottom right: *I was at school when my mother took me to see Godfrey for the first time. He was playing Antony in* Antony and Cleopatra. *Kenneth Tynan described his performance as "still an eager warrior . . . like the man in Bunyan, he would hack his way into heaven, after giving and receiving many wounds. About him legends would gather and multiply . . . such playing asks for a monument."*
Left: *Godfrey and Katharine Cornell in* Antony and Cleopatra *in New York, described as "two ancient*

sports" by an American schoolboy.

Above: *Godfrey in the film* The Beginning or the End *in which he plays Roosevelt. Godfrey's likeness to the great man was very strong. Sometimes when I cross Grosvenor Square, I find myself inclined to stop for a word with the statue.*
Left: *Godfrey's first Othello at the Royal Court was as long ago as 1921. W. A. Darlington wrote that in the role Godfrey "reached a giant's stature". But it was eleven years before anybody offered him another chance to play in Shakespeare.*

113

Two Stratford seasons.
Top: *Godfrey, Othello,
1948. He directed. He played the role again the following year.*
Right: *With Diana
Wynyard as his Desdemona,
a woman of integrity, beauty
and brains.*
Opposite: *With Anthony
Quayle as a brilliant Iago
(top left). Godfrey as Macbeth. Anthony Quayle
directed. It was the play
which opened the 1949 season (top right).*
*Leon Quartermaine as Ban-
quo with me as his son
Fleance – the part I did not
wish to play (bottom).*

Top: A Midsummer Night's Dream, *directed by Michael Benthall. I am the fairy (right) in a long blonde wig.*

Above: Cymbeline, *directed by Michael Benthall. I am on the left among the Court ladies. I thought walking on very boring.*

Right: *The Banquet Scene in* Macbeth.

Opposite: *Some of our things on the Cornish holiday. Godfrey's beloved sailing books, one of them on the subject of knots. A photograph which I took of him on the boat. His pipe. A silver kettle (I used it to make the tea). And a wildly expensive Asprey's cocktail shaker.*

Godfrey in the snow on Christmas Day in Cornwall. The photograph I took of him on his cutter the Barbara Mary.

116

Left: *My favourite picture of Godfrey. It was at the Café de Paris where he had taken me to see Noël Coward. I cut myself out of the picture because I thought I looked dreadful. Godfrey was furious with me for doing that.*

Below and opposite top right: *Godfrey in* The Heiress, *with Wendy Hiller, Haymarket, 1950. They took over from Ralph Richardson and Peggy Ashcroft; John Gielgud directed.*

Opposite: *In one of my dreaded maid roles with Tony Britton (top left).*

As Sam Weller's girl in Pickwick Papers, *one of my roles as a servant (middle). With Peter Finch and Diana Wynyard in* Captain Carvallo *(bottom).*

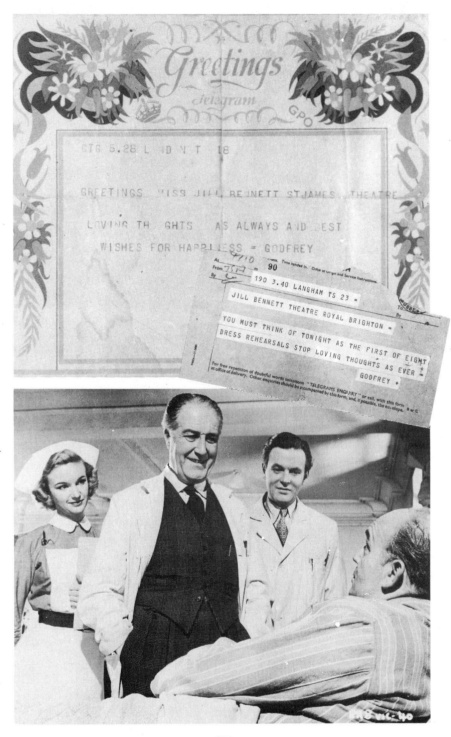

Opposite: *Two first night telegrams which Godfrey sent me. The second telegram came when I was touring in* A Fiddle at the Wedding, *by Penelope Pakenham Walsh, directed by Peter Ustinov. We were booed at Streatham, and the play never reached London. I was the second juvenile, the butler's daughter.*

Godfrey's bedside manner in White Corridors. *Moira Lister and Jack Watling look on.*

Top left: *With Mary Kerridge in* His House in Order.

Top right: *The first time I was ever painted – a portrait by Frances Marshall, 1952.*

Left: *Godfrey in Pinero's* His House in Order, *New Theatre, 1951. He had beautiful hands, and always used them in his photographs – they were very expressive.*

R119-122

Opposite: The Titfield Thunderbolt, *a lovely role for Godfrey, funny and full of character and a marvellous film.* Top and bottom right: *Godfrey and George Relph. Godfrey loved trains, and George Relph.* Bottom left: *A picture I took of Godfrey in the West Country while* The Titfield Thunderbolt *was being filmed – Godfrey is only partly dressed for his role as the Bishop; he's wearing his own jacket.*

Top: *In John Huston's* Moulin Rouge, *as the barmaid. I had six lines and filmed for thirty days.*

Left: *Godfrey, winter 1952, in* The Hanging Judge, *adapted by Raymond Massey. Godfrey loved the part. He knew a good many judges; he met them at the Garrick and some of them were close friends.*

123

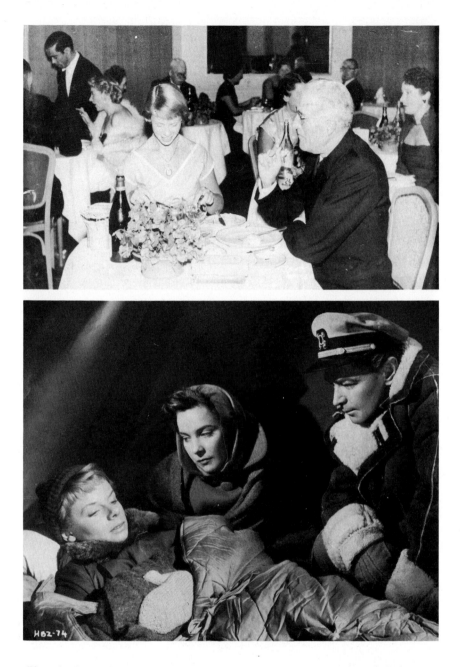

The only photograph which I have of us together, taken while we were in Madeira during the holiday he so disliked because he was very ill. I used to eat to make him believe I was happy and relaxed.

Above and opposite top: *My first good film role, in* Hell Below Zero, *opposite Alan Ladd.*

Opposite left: *Two publicity stills from* Hell Below Zero: *I was pleased with my hair which I cut with nail scissors; at the wheel of the ship.*

Above: *A silver dressing-table set, with my name engraved in Godfrey's writing, was one of the presents he gave me.*

Top: *A publicity picture
taken while I was filming*
Hell Below Zero, *showing
me as a gamine film star.*
Above: *The last picture of
Godfrey, taken very soon
before he died.*
Two pictures from Time
Present: *Pamela, talking
about Orme after having
visited him in hospital;
Pamela refuses to go to his
funeral.*

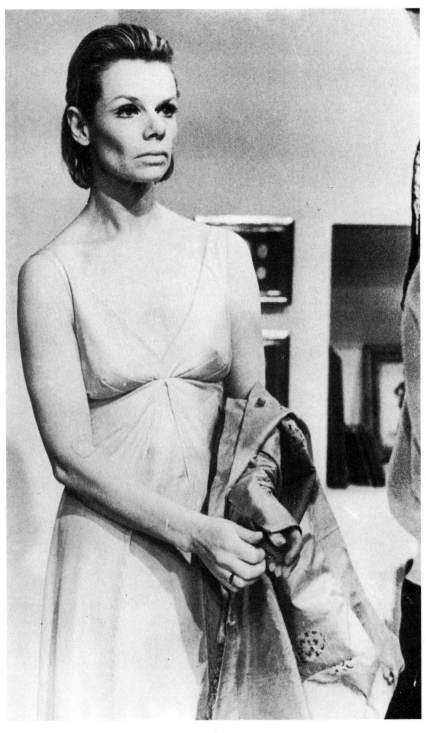

DUKE OF YORK'S THEATRE

St. Martin's Lane, W.C.2   Telephone TEM 5122

Licensed by the Lord Chamberlain to EDWARD HORAN   Managing Agents: THEATRE MANAGERS LIMITED

The English Stage Company and Lewenstein-Delfont Productions Limited .

JILL BENNETT
TIME PRESENT
JOHN OSBORNE

FOR A LIMITED SEASON

spoke in that way. When one sees films of the period, the clothes look odd and interesting, but it is the accents which jar. They sound so ludicrously affected.

Diana showed her low opinion of me as an actress, but Laurence Olivier never did. Another director would have thrown me out. I knew I wasn't any good and kept expecting the sack. But instead of telling me I was bad and must get better he actually said I was good. Godfrey once told me about Mrs. Patrick Campbell in Pinero's *The Second Mrs. Tanquerary*, and the story illustrates something Laurence Olivier knew – the power of encouragement. On the opening night when the play started Pinero and the producer Dion Bouccicault were appalled at her performance. During the interval they went to see her in her dressing-room – and told her she was brilliant. They had previously agreed there was nothing to lose by this whopping lie, she was so awful she couldn't get worse. "Go on," they said, "you've got the audience in the palm of your hand. The evening is yours." For the rest of the play she was superb.

I certainly wasn't as the sulky maid, but Olivier's encouragement, his assuring me that I could do it and that I was good, did work. When we were touring before the play opened in London, he sent me a marvellous letter which I still treasure. "Try to remember that acting is only a game. But a game which has to be won."

Captain Carvallo opened in Glasgow, where I shared digs with Richard Goolden, an eccentric, clever, sweet little man like an amiable gnome, best known to generations of children for his performance as the dear timid Mole in *Toad of Toad Hall*. He loved chatting to actresses and he and I became friends. Our friendship was to last for the rest of his life. Richard talked about Godfrey, and told me a story of when Godfrey was the first president of Equity. He asked Richard to become a member. Richard refused.

"I'm truly sorry, Godfrey. But I'm afraid I can't join a Union. It would interfere with my feeling for God."

Godfrey waived Richard's subscription and conveniently forgot all about the conversation. I never knew if Richard eventually did become a member of Equity.

During the tour, when we played in Bournemouth, for instance, I hurried back to London to spend my Sundays with Godfrey. Sometimes he drove me to my next date, taking me down on Sunday night or early on Monday morning before returning for his own performance. We drove in the Dolomite, wrapped up in warm clothes and driving with the hood down. In London Godfrey had a woman chauffeur who drove him about in a hired car.

It was a blessing that I had Laurence Olivier's letter to read and re-read. One afternoon at the matinee in Brighton, when the curtain went up at the start of the play and there I was, doing my desultory sweeping of the floor, an old lady in the front stalls said in a deafening whisper,

"What a very plain girl. I hope we're not going to see much of *her.*"

In those days not only in the theatre but in the world, the idea of feminine good looks had not changed since the days when Gladys Cooper reigned. Hers was a classic beauty which can still be seen, a golden vision, in a full length portrait of her by John Collier in the Garrick Club. Gamines used to be regarded as plain or even ugly. This was before Audrey Hepburn proved that high cheekbones and a big mouth could belong to a woman as well as to an elf, and thus changed the look of women. Of course Katharine Hepburn and Bette Davis were neither of them beauties in the old-fashioned sense; but they were great stars with all the unreality and power created round them by Hollywood. In England there was only one kind of accepted beauty – the English rose, with a flawless oval face and a straight nose. Members of my own family thought in that way, my aunt once remarking to my mother, "Jill will never make an actress, she is far too plain." Godfrey liked my looks. He told me I was attractive, but I didn't think so. If you are unusual-looking you always thirst to look exactly like everybody else. It's the same with personality. The very thing about you which makes you different is the one that you despise.

Captain Carvallo opened at the St. James's in August 1950. It was high summer in London, dusty and hot. I didn't enjoy the first night performance. I didn't, in fact, enjoy being in the play at all although it was my first real London appearance (I do not count *Pickwick*). I had quite a sweet little love scene in *Carvallo*, but only a few lines, and I still hadn't learned the trick of enjoying a small part. Some actors actually prefer a small part; they like to come on and shine, and then teasingly disappear. But I couldn't and didn't.

Tanya Moiseiwitsch designed the play, which looked ravishing. It was the first time I was playing a part of any significance and met an important designer, for as Bianca I had worn the costume of another actress. Nothing was too much trouble for Tanya, who taught me how to tie my kerchief and how to make it settle so that it looked right and felt comfortable. Her costumes were wonderful to wear as well as to look at.

Roger Furse, a great friend of Laurence Olivier and one of the directors of Laurence Olivier Productions, had invited the whole company to his home for a first night party; I decided beforehand that I was not going to go. I was too nervous. And in any case the leading actor, James Donald, had taken a dislike to me. He was really unpleasant to me whenever he got the chance. I found it puzzling and depressing. Why go to the party?

After the performance Godfrey collected me at the stage door, and took me round the corner for a quick supper at the Caprice. During the meal he said,

"You have to go to the party, you know."

"No, I won't. I don't want to."

"But you must."

He had not been invited and that did not bother him. He told me that it would be graceless to refuse and was not – he knew me well – at all professional. So I went. The party was given in a very grand studio flat near Cheyne Walk and to my surprise I enjoyed myself.

Godfrey didn't see me in the play for a long time, because he was playing every night too, and we only had Sundays free. When he finally managed to see the play, I don't think he thought I was very good. Sadly, it was not until after he died that I began to play anything that really suited me and showed my paces.

Our life together was never to a fixed pattern. We came and went. We used the town, we went out or we sat at home eating Godfrey's favourite food which, apart from Haddock Monte Carlo, was cod with caper sauce. When I think of us together, that big, easy, autocratic worldly man and me, I know it was the easiest relationship I have ever had in my life. He gave me what people now call tender loving care and support. That was what I was given and I am not sure what I gave in return except my love. I wasn't frightened about him and me, he was one of the few men in my life who did not make me feel anxious.

Sometimes when his friends invited him out, he would say "May I bring my friend, Jill Bennett?" Godfrey always used my full name when introducing me or speaking about me. Hearing that made me feel like a real actress and gave me extra self-respect. There were times when his friends said – of course, do bring her. But at other times they tactfully said they would prefer to see him alone. That didn't mean Godfrey did not accept the invitation. I went home to my parents and I never once waited for the telephone to ring. I didn't think a lot about us, I just knew we were what I thought of as "all right". It is later when life has betrayed you, when you've been deeply unhappy over family or love, money or work, that you lose your feeling of safety. I was utterly safe then. I suppose we must have been slightly out of joint with ordinary life or we would never have chosen each other. We didn't want what we were expected to want: he, a dashing woman. Me, a conventional young man.

Godfrey was great friends with my mother now, and he and my father liked each other very much. I realise I've said nothing about my father. I didn't really get to know him, because during those important years of late childhood and early teens, I was in England and he was in a Japanese prisoner-of-war camp. He was very ill while he was a prisoner, and he did not come home for two and a half years after the war ended. His life had been torn into two. His work in Penang was gone, he had lost all his money, and his health was broken by the time we met again. He was a very quiet man, reserved and gentle, utterly unlike the actors I mixed with. He was clever, and it sounds exaggerated to say that I saw him as noble. Like a character in a Somerset Maugham book about the Far East, whom he much resembled, he could drink anybody under the table. He never drank wine, it was gin, with water waved over it as Americans wave the martini bottle over the gin. He drank whisky during his meals. His capacity was incredible and I never saw him drunk in my life. While he sat quietly drinking his gin, my mother had a White Lady. People don't drink cocktails much nowadays, and a White Lady is a rare and delicious concoction. It is made of two parts gin, a part Cointreau and a part fresh lemon juice, but my mother had her own version. She had champagne as well as gin.

When *Captain Carvallo* ended there was a short break. Nothing lengthy; Laurence Olivier had no time for players taking long holidays. Then we were to appear in a double bill, Shaw's *Caesar and Cleopatra* and Shakespeare's *Antony and Cleopatra*. Vivien Leigh was to play Shaw's kitten and Shakespeare's ageing sorceress. Olivier would play Caesar and – Godfrey's great success – Antony.

Olivier gave me the part of Iras in both plays. She has nothing to do in Shaw but stand about and giggle, but in Shakespeare, Iras, one of Cleopatra's attendants, has real character. That was something, I thought. She also has two lines which everybody in the world knows –

> Finish, good lady; the bright day is done,
> And we are for the dark.

I wasn't entranced with my two parts although I knew I ought to be grateful for being given them.

Godfrey's play had closed, but there was a film comedy at Ealing coming up soon, *I Believe in You*, in which he would be playing with Cecil Parker. There was just time for us – it was early spring in 1951 – to have a short holiday. Godfrey decided upon Spain. He had recently lunched at Buck's Club with his friend Herbert Buckmaster, who had told him about a quiet still-undiscovered coastal village called Fuengirola, near Malaga. It would be, said Buck, just the thing. Godfrey wanted to know if there was a good hotel, by which he naturally meant a splendid one. Yes, said Buck, there certainly was but that was all there was. A beach and a splendid hotel.

Godfrey invited my parents to come with us to Spain. My father was not well enough, and in any case couldn't bear the idea of leaving England. My mother looked pleased and accepted. The three of us set off together. We spent the night in Gibraltar, and arrived in Fuengirola the next day. Herbert Buckmaster had not exaggerated; it was an extremely grand hotel overlooking a wide sandy beach and the peaceful Mediterranean. My mother spoke good French, and Godfrey like the fine actor he was could act in any language, including what appeared to be a fluent Spanish sign language. My schoolgirl French was nowhere so I left it to the others to do the talking.

Fuengirola was utterly quiet, a world of sand and sea, with an ancient fortress, and pines and palms which went down to the water's edge. It was winter and quite cold, and my mother and I often went for long walks on the beach, striding on the sands in cold sunlight, talking animatedly, and rarely meeting a soul. Although the air was chill, Godfrey and I couldn't resist swimming. It was the first time we had swum together since we had braved the rough Cornish rollers. I had tennis lessons, playing with a coach . . .

It was a relaxed, united kind of holiday. I enjoyed being with Godfrey and my mother at the same time. The idea of it being difficult to share either of them didn't enter my mind. We got on well. There was not much to do, but none of us was restless. Godfrey hired a car so that we could go on his favourite kind of expedition, one with a purpose. To see the watch towers built to guard the coast from pirates, for instance. Or to look at the orange groves or the sugar plantations. To visit Malaga. I had passed my test by now and the three of us took turns to drive. When the sun came out, the light was cold and the sky was coloured like an opal. Across the dry rocky country, we saw ruined castles sometimes on the skyline. We didn't always get to where we had planned; we always enjoyed ourselves.

The hotel was rather empty, except for a few Spanish families. After dinner in the evenings, the three of us sat and talked. We always meant to have an early night and we always stayed up very late . . .

"It would be nice," Godfrey said, when the holiday was almost over, "if we could have a couple of days more."

With difficulty because of the uncertain Spanish telephone exchange, he finally managed to telephone Laurence Olivier.

"Would it be possible for Jill Bennett to be two days late for rehearsal?" he asked, using his most charming manner.

The answer was brief.

"No."

Six

The two plays, the Shaw and the Shakespeare, which were soon to be known as the Two Cleopatras, were part of the 1951 Festival of Britain. They had never been presented together before, and they gave Laurence Olivier and Vivien Leigh powerful and fascinating roles – Olivier as Shaw's worldly-wise sardonic Caesar, and Shakespeare's ageing lover who thinks the world well lost for love; Vivien Leigh alternating Shaw's sixteen year old Egyptian minx with Shakespeare's sorceress of the Nile. And it was to be the first time the Oliviers were acting together, in their own company and in their own theatre.

I had, of course, studied both my roles. Iras in Shaw was nothing, a mere looker-on. In Shakespeare, as one of Cleopatra's two devoted attendants who dies with her queen, Iras has only a dozen or so lines, despite two of them being immortal. I did love rehearsals, and found it fascinating to watch Laurence Olivier and Vivien Leigh together. She worked intensely hard, with a passionate determination to get things right. She also created a happy atmosphere, everybody in the company loved her, she was friendly and kind as well as beautiful. It is curious to remember her rehearsing. She wore such formal clothes; slender high-heeled shoes, jewellery, even a hat. Once I saw Margaret Leighton walking down King Street towards the St. James's Theatre on her way to rehearse *Separate Tables*. She wore a black Dior suit, a large black hat, and gloves. When I rehearsed the two parts in the same Rattigan plays, years later, I wore jeans and a T shirt. Rehearsal rooms are usually filthy, and actors spend most of their time on the floor, for the director is bound to say "Would you do that fall again?"

The clothes we once wore at rehearsals were absurd, but the joy was the same. I absolutely love rehearsing – I learn so much. I have begun to enjoy the actual performances more than I used to do, but rehearsals have always been special. My idea of real pleasure is to rehearse in a draughty old drill hall, with a wonderful director and cast, and simply go on for ever, with no opening night. Lindsay Anderson said to me not long ago at the end of a rehearsal, "Be better tomorrow." Instead of feeling cast down, I was positively encouraged and buoyant when he said that.

Michael Benthall was directing both Cleopatra plays. He choreographed them with skill, and Olivier had a seductive hand in them without you exactly noticing that it was there. At the first rehearsal Michael greeted me with a "Hello, it's Fairy Fraught."

I was brought up to be punctual by my mother; when she said she would be somewhere at a certain time she always arrived early. Punctuality is what I respect and I never sympathise with, in fact rather despise, people who are consistently late. I have something in common with Egyptian women who, when they arrange to meet a man, arrive as the clock strikes the hour and if he is not there waiting, simply drive or walk away.

With my passion for being on time I was horrified when I arrived late for one of the rehearsals. Laurence Olivier saw me creeping in and fixed me with a mesmeric eye.

"Don't do that again. Or you'll be sacked."

On the following morning he was caught in a nightmarish traffic jam outside Buckingham Palace and arrived very late himself. He came onstage looking tense, took one look at me and put his hand to his forehead.

"What can I say?"

Our costumes for *Antony and Cleopatra*, designed by Audrey Cruddas, consisted of a kind of rubbery stuff smeared over our naked bodies in the making process and then left to set into our shapes. It had a most disgusting smell, and, to say the least, was inconvenient if your shape was like mine and changing all the time, skinny one week and plump the next. When the costumes had set into moulds, Vivien looked glorious and all the other women looked awful. I had a wig quite as bad as the one I never wore as Bianca; this one was made of yellow string. I detested it, and all wigs. I used to puzzle over why Vivien's wig looked so very different from everyone else's. I didn't know that *she* went to an entirely different place, that she knew what she was doing and what she wanted. I've learned a lot about wigs since then, about what they can do for you when you're creating a part. And who makes superb ones.

The plays received great acclaim and I settled down to my two Irases, Shaw's silent one and Shakespeare's with the few (if unforgettable) lines. My old friend Edmund Purdom had not yet gone, trailing stardust, to Hollywood. He played the messenger who is whipped by Cleopatra. He was still the same handsome man, still more interested in inventing drinks or cooking luscious meals than in his career. Vivien disliked him because he was lazy and relied on his good looks, didn't work and was more interested in making the tea.

During a performance of *Antony* a startling thing happened: the revolve which changed one set to the next was wrongly switched. When Cleopatra and her attendants entered what was supposed to be the Egyptian Court, they found themselves among the pillars of Rome. Here was Cleopatra exclaiming that a messenger had come from Italy when we were there all the time. Vivien stayed cool as a cucumber during the scene. Afterwards the poor stagehand came, sweating, to apologise. She put her hand on his arm and laughed, quoting Rhett Butler, "Darling, I don't give a dam'."

Vivien was enchanting to me during the season at the St. James's. She was a restless, exciting woman, much more complicated than she seemed, a real enchantress. She was very beautiful, every feature was perfect, yet that didn't make her face seem lifeless, it was vulnerable and changeable and full of feeling. At the end of *Antony*, before Iras falls and dies, Cleopatra kisses her and then says "Have I the aspic on my lips?" Vivien always kissed me passionately. Laurence Olivier was amused, and used to stand in the wings timing the kiss.

I was working, and in good spirits, and it was just about then that I first met Lindsay Anderson. We played together in an art film *The Pleasure Garden* by James Broughton. The film was made at Crystal Palace and Gavin Lambert directed. Lindsay played the hero, a boy who falls in love with a plain girl who pretends to be a beautiful statue. It was an odd, fey kind of piece – I remember in the film that Lindsay and I went together to the woods, where I sat domestically sewing on his buttons. We got 7s. 6d. each for our performances. Lindsay has become one of my closest and most loyal friends. His work exactly reflects him – he has vision, an epic view. I always think of him as utterly un-English. He is the best, the fiercest kind of Scot.

Godfrey came to see me in *Antony*, and told me that he liked the way I said my lines. But although I did well, the part was not a challenge. He knew I was restless, longing to work harder. In Godfrey's day you played a hundred parts in a year, that was how you learned your job. But to be in a long run with a very small part is frustrating when you are young. You're in a success. Yet it isn't yours.

Godfrey admired the production and the performances very much, although Antony had been one of his own greatest roles. I noticed often, and with wonder, his lack of jealousy. Most actors if they are truthful will admit to a pang when somebody else takes a success of theirs and turns it into his own. But Godfrey genuinely liked to see other actors hit the heights. He simply knew that he was good too. Peter Hall once said that Godfrey's was the best Antony he had ever seen.

When Godfrey was playing the role in New York, with Katharine Cornell as his Cleopatra, they made a great romantic entrance at the start of the play. Cleopatra spoke her first lines, "If it be love, indeed, tell me how much," and Godfrey came rushing on to the stage carrying her in his arms.

When the first night was over he said to her,

"I've been thinking. Perhaps we'd better walk on instead."

"Oh Godfrey! But why?"

"Because I'm too old and you're too heavy."

During the run, a class of New York schoolchildren were given a general knowledge paper to do. Among the questions was "Name two ancient sports."

One child wrote, "Godfrey Tearle and Katharine Cornell."

Godfrey had a big reputation in New York and the Americans loved him. He'd worked a lot in the States in the theatre, had filmed in Hollywood, and in any case he was half American. I used to think he had the easy American manner and that there was a transatlantic flavour to his voice. He said "Tearrle here," on the telephone, rolling his 'r's in the American way, and it was always "Corn*wall*," with the last syllable lengthened. When we were in London, a succession of friends from America turned up to see him and dine with us.

"Godfrey's hot property in New York," one friend told me. "But not so hot on casting. When he auditioned Claudette Colbert he said she was a rotten actress and turned her down."

"Ah," said Godfrey, "but I took her out to dinner."

The St. James's was a beautiful theatre and I loved it. Now it's lost for ever. Vivien Leigh organised a march to save it, when she knew it was to be demolished. It had been the theatre where she had her first big success, at twenty-one, in a play called *The Mask of Virtue*. There was a tradition that the St. James's was haunted by George Alexander, a gentle ghost, checking to see people were in their dressing-rooms and everything was ready for the curtain to go up. I never met him. I wish I had.

Godfrey was now playing at the New Theatre in Pinero's *His House in Order*. The piece hadn't been seen in the West End for many years. Originally it had been a great star vehicle for Irene Vanbrugh as a girl, a slave to her parents-in-law, who breaks out and wins her freedom. A New Woman. The Vanbrugh part was now played by Mary Kerridge, and Godfrey was the man she confides in, a kind of father confessor. Godfrey told me he was too old for the role, that the character shouldn't be more than forty. I thought he was marvellous. He had known the Edwardian world and he had its essence and its style.

We were both playing every night now, and met, he and I, like other busy actors, for poached eggs at the Buckstone Club in a basement opposite the Stage door of the Haymarket Theatre. I was working hard (despite wanting more to do) and was cheerful. I love hard work, it suits me, just as I detest desultory work, coffee breaks, coming in late and leaving at five. It must have been a relief to Godfrey that I'd stopped saying my career was over. Poor Godfrey, I could be very boring, and he did not hesitate to tell me so. The trouble was that I did not always shut up when I should have done.

I was his constant companion, but he liked to see other people, perhaps as a rest from me. He and Margaret Leighton often lunched together; they were friends before Godfrey and I met. She was tall and angular, with a quirky eccentric sort of manner which was apparent in her playing. Her face was striking, she had very blue eyes, and there were odd, unexpected tones in her voice. Her performances had edge, but although she could be very sharp, you always knew that she had heart. Godfrey told me he thought her marvellous. He cut a photograph of her out of the *Tatler* and put it on the mantelpiece, saying "Now there's somebody who is a real actress." I was very gritty about that but it had no effect. He told me not to be stupid.

I went out with other people too. I still knew a number of young men, ex Guards officers, gentlemen farmers, men who had been in the war. Some were quite poor, and others had that quiet unmistakable air of being rich. To Godfrey I called them the Hooray Henrys. Some of the Henrys had come down to Stratford when I was there. They were all totally ignorant of the theatre and astonished that I was not playing Desdemona and Lady Macbeth. They didn't get the theatre. They did understand horses, and most of them were marvellous dancers.

Various Hooray Henrys took me dancing to the Four Hundred. It was dark and romantic, the music was good, and people went there to sit pressed close, or dance even closer, but I simply liked dancing for its own sake. My companions in their late twenties never seemed as young as Godfrey. He was like Picasso, who once said that "To be young, really young, takes a very, very long time."

Sometimes the Henrys drove me home to my parents' flat, and sometimes I went back to Queen Anne Street. Once, at about four in the morning, I let myself into Godfrey's flat, crept into his room in my ball gown, and moved about deliberately making its skirts swish.

Godfrey opened one eye.

"It's all right. I'm awake. Did you have a good time?"

"Not bad."

"Like a glass of champagne?"

"I didn't mean to wake you —" I lied.

"Didn't you? Get yourself a glass and mix me a martini while you're about it. I thought you were going home tonight."

"I was. I changed my mind."

We saw each other as much as we could. He gave me treats . . . we went to the Moulin d'Or, for instance. It was a lovely restaurant where theatre people used to meet, owned by two brothers. The daughter of one of them worked at the St. James's. But the treats became rare because Godfrey was so busy. He was filming again, making *Mandy*, the film about teaching a little deaf child to talk, with Jack Hawkins, Phyllis Calvert and Mandy Miller. Someone else was in the cast: his old flame Gladys Cooper. They had not filmed together for years; Godfrey had been in love with her once.

Our loving friendship was going well because I was working and did not inflict my glooms on him. He disapproved of them and said they were destructive and got in the way of my life. He didn't like my spinsterish side either, because he had one himself. He saw me realistically, despite our affection, and I had moments of criticising *him*. He had such high ideals that I thought him a bit of a prig. He disliked bad language, which always made me laugh. I did think, too, that he should not let people treat him badly sometimes. He ought to be more difficult. But that was his nature. Kenneth Tynan wrote about Godfrey that he was "positively the kindliest actor in the world". Godfrey did not like that at all. Certain roles, certain mantles seemed to be put on Godfrey. But he knew exactly what he was doing. He was far, far tougher than he chose to appear.

He told me, at about that time, that he had been asked if he would be knighted in the Birthday Honours.

"I've turned it down twice," he said.

"Then why accept now?" I asked disapprovingly, being in my Marxist phase at the time.

"I don't know . . . it would be useful to get us good cinema seats. And Olive would like it."

Olive Harding was his agent and a great friend.

So it was Olive who went to Buckingham Palace to see Godfrey being made a Sir, not me.

Just as we had done at Stratford when we had any free time from work, we went on expeditions. We drove out to the country on Sundays, to the Bull at Gerrard's Cross or the Bear at Woodstock. We went to Brighton and walked on the pier and had dinner at the Old Ship. We picnicked. We sang. I made him laugh, which was something I never found difficult. One day at lunch he suddenly said,

"I suppose I shall have to marry you. Do you fancy being Lady Tearle?"

"Not much."

There was a pause. He appeared to be waiting, and I added, "Anyway, you said you enjoy being free."

"Yes. I do."

If he was being selfish to enjoy his independence, so was I. And how did I know it was going to last? When he annoyed me, or when I felt things were dull, I used to think – perhaps I don't love this fellow. Once when I was offended by some stupid thing I said seriously,

"I don't think I love you any more."

He looked at me sardonically.

"Funny. Because I haven't loved you for the last two days. However. That isn't something you should say to somebody until you've thought it over. We both will. If we wait forty-eight hours it may change."

I was crestfallen by this crushing remark. Things didn't seem to be going the way I planned.

I did behave badly quite often. I sulked because I was trying not to have it out, whatever "it" was at the time. I waited for things to blow over, and I've never been any good at that. I would sooner clear the air and know the worst at once. When we quarrelled there were times, they were rare, when he showed his temper. It hardly ever happened for he was amazingly self-controlled, but when it did he was alarming, and then we both exploded. Once when we had a quarrel which Godfrey considered was at an end, and I didn't, he took a taxi to the Garrick Club. I followed him. I marched through the sacred portals into the hallowed place where women in those days were only allowed on Sundays. It was a weekday. I told the shocked porter that I must see Mr. Tearle. I had previously decided never to call him Sir Godfrey. Godfrey came down the flight of stairs two at a time absolutely furious, took hold of my wrist, sat down and put me across his knee. He really spanked me. Then threw me into a taxi, saying "Go home and learn to behave yourself."

I was extremely well behaved for a day or two. He was not deceived, and I caught that eye on me with the same look he had worn when he watched me playing Bianca.

In the autumn of 1951 the celebrations for the Festival of Britain were finishing, and we were told that the Two Cleopatras would be going to New York. I made up my mind that I wouldn't go too. I had played the parts for nine months and knew in my soul that I couldn't do them any better. I didn't think – whoops, I'll go to New York and have a terrific time and take my pay and play Iras with my hands tied behind my back. I was bored with Iras, it was already behind me. My idea was to get on, and getting on is not hanging on. It is sometimes important to be out of work and open to offers. Besides, you can't go on being fascinated by saying a dozen or so lines a night for months. Unless the part is very big, you can't try to make it fresh every night. Long runs, in any case, have never suited me, my ideal work is in one of the repertory theatres. I didn't want to go to America, I wasn't going to play safe. I was very decisive in those days. I also did not want to leave Godfrey. Laurence Olivier and Vivien Leigh were both wonderfully kind when I told them I would not be coming on the tour. I think perhaps *they* knew that if either of them had been me, they would have done the same.

Giving up being a member of Laurence Olivier's company was rash, but I have never been cautious in work. I'm cautious in love and friendship, though. My sign is Capricorn but it is close to Sagittarius. Although the goat sounds a plodding animal, he is quick and agile, darting up or down a sheer slope with his little high-heeled feet. Perhaps I wasn't cautious about love either, when I was young. I've become so because I've had to learn that people are not as nice as you think they are.

In the spring Godfrey made another film, *The Titfield Thunderbolt* directed by Charles Crichton (who did another famous Ealing comedy, *The Lavender Hill Mob*). It was to be shot on location in the west country and I went down to Bath to join him in a hotel for ten days while he was filming. The weather was beautiful, and it was fun driving out into the country early in the morning with Godfrey, to watch the interesting chaos of film-making; particularly when Douglas Slocombe took an hour and a half to choose and light a tree. How patient everybody was. As a matter of fact I had made my first real film the previous year, but mine had been a somewhat instant performance. I played a chorus girl who was murdered in the first reel. In fact I think my entire performance was over while the credits were rolling. The murder was filmed at the stage door of the old Lyric Theatre, Hammersmith, and we shot at night when the show at the theatre was over. The film, *The Long Dark Hall*, was not much praised. Leslie Halliwell described it as "a miserable mystery with a trick ending". It starred Rex Harrison and Lilli Palmer, and Rex had not been very sure that he would choose me. He said my nose was like a potato.

The Titfield Thunderbolt was an Ealing comedy about a railway, the story of a group of villagers determined to save their branch line, and the astonishingly resourceful way they go about it. The film had a cast of wonderful English comedians – Stanley Holloway, George Relph, Hugh Griffith, Naunton Wayne. Stanley used to sing us songs from the days when he was a player at the end of the pier. One song he and Godfrey sang together was something about "three hundred and sixty five days, All go to make a year". Godfrey played a bishop in the film, and was nicknamed by everybody "the bishop of Orson Welles". There was a scene in which the bishop helps to drive an ancient locomotive. Gradually he peels off one piece of his dignified clerical vestments after the other . . . he has wanted to drive a train ever since he was a small boy. Godfrey's performance was a joy. It was to be his last film.

When you are filming, life – to say the least – is

simplified. You must be up at six in the morning, and after the day's work, when you come home, you're glad to be in bed as early as possible. I didn't see much of Godfrey in consequence. But I hung about watching the film, and a girl friend came down to stay and keep me company. Sometimes I went out for a drink in the evening with the camera crew.

My dates for some of the work Godfrey or I did at that time may be wrong, for we were two people with acting careers. But whereas Godfrey's career always rushed along swiftly and he was in constant demand, mine often ground to a halt. But I think just about then I was sent for by John Huston.

The summons came quite out of the blue. I did not even know he had ever seen me. As it turned out, he hadn't. But one of his friends had – in *Pickwick* of all things. I knew he was now casting for a new film, *Moulin Rouge*, a life of Toulouse-Lautrec, from Pierre la Mure's novel. I arrived in a Soho Square office and was introduced to Huston. I saw a big, haggard, humorous man who had a slow manner and heavy-lidded clever eyes.

"I'm very interested in you," he said.

I just sat, hardly daring to breathe. Jack Clayton was his assistant and Huston turned to him.

"Is there anything in the movie for this girl?"

"Nothing, I'm afraid, Mr. Huston."

"Then we've got to find something for her."

John Huston looked at me again and said something that I have heard very often, and which people rarely mean.

"Trust me," he said. He added that he was going to find something for me because "I'd like to put your face on the screen."

They made a part specially for me: I was the Renoir girl in a scene based on *The Bar at the Folies Bergères*. I was quite unlike the painting, but that did not seem to

149

bother them, in fact it interested them. I did not even wear the same clothes . . . but the effect, that was what John Huston aimed at. He was not going to show the audience a photograph of Renoir's painting, a reproduction. He wanted to bring the barmaid to life. He was using a new Technicolor process for the film, and an expert came over from Hollywood to advise about that. When they filmed my scene in the bar, they used clouds of smoke to get the blurred, hazy effect of the painting. I had six lines to speak, and thirty-two glorious days of work, including having to ride in a hunting scene, dressed as a boy.

When Godfrey and I spent our evenings in Queen Anne Street, I always asked him to tell me more about the past. He didn't live in the past, he was never nostalgic, he was too busy and too interested in the present. But sometimes in conversation he would mention an actor, Henry Ainley for instance, and then he would say "You don't know anything about him, do you?"

"Not much. Tell me."

Godfrey leaned back in his chair and the story started.

He had played in his father's company in the provinces until Osmond Tearle died when Godfrey was seventeen. Godfrey inherited the responsibility of the company, and coolly took them to South Africa, where they stayed for two years. He played in an enormous variety of plays, from the classics to Edwardian nonsense, and had a whale of a time, including a love affair with a woman of sixty. "But the manager," he said, "got me out of that."

As a young man he was remarkably handsome. Everybody thought so except Godfrey, who worried about his legs which he thought were too thin. He padded them to make them look muscular. Just as a flat-chested woman is convinced that the only part of her anybody will look at is her breasts, Godfrey worried about the shape of his legs. His good looks were a hindrance to him in a way. He did not have to work all that hard, and although he strove he was never driven. The fact that I was never a beauty meant that I have always had to work to make audiences believe that I am. Godfrey's looks were only praised.

He was quite pleased to get older, he said. Getting slightly bald made him look more clever.

"You would have loathed me when I was young. My hair grew too near my eyebrows."

He enjoyed the life of an actor, and played as many as fifty different roles during the two years he was in South Africa. He wasn't lazy, but acting came easily, and all his life he could give an impression of careless rapture, of nobility. He played heroes, not cads. Acting when Godfrey was young was not heavy or introverted, and actors were not prepared for a production in advance by a kind of psychiatrist's meeting. I enjoy all that, but it was not Godfrey's way or the way of any actor at that time. They learned a part, banged it about during very short rehearsals, and simply went out on to the stage and did it. He played with zest. All his life, he took whatever parts came to hand, some wonderful and some dreadful, and played them with his whole self.

I was trained to think – and then to speak. But Albert Finney once said to me: "Sometimes I'm sure it is best to think and speak at the same time." And Lindsay Anderson has said to me – "Don't hesitate. Go on. *Just say it.*"

That was what Godfrey always did.

In South Africa women began to fall in love with the young English actor. They wrote him love letters. They stood in the broiling heat at the stage door, waiting for him to sign their programmes. One evening a wealthy-looking man came to the theatre and asked for him. He was shown into Godfrey's dressing-room.

"Well, Mr. Tearle. I'm here to say that I've seen you a number of times, and I want to put you under contract."

Godfrey was interested.

"To act where?" he asked.

"No, no, nothing to do with acting," said his visitor. "I'd like to put you under contract for stud purposes."

Godfrey! That most innocent and puritanical of men.

When he eventually returned to England, he took his company around the provinces on tour, as Osmond had done. I never asked him why that did not last, but it can't have succeeded for later he joined a repertory company. There was not a familiar part in the classics which Godfrey did not play at that time. Romeo, Shylock, Brutus, Sir Peter Teazle. He played a ridiculously young Othello. That must have been strangely different to the Othello I had watched so often from the wings at Stratford.

While he was in the provinces he met an actress called Mary Plante, who had changed her name for the stage to Mary Malone. Perhaps she thought an Irish name was romantic. She was very attractive, and Godfrey, aged twenty, proposed to her when they were on tour, at Crewe I think. I had the impression that he asked her to marry him because he felt that he ought to; she was the first girl he had ever been serious about. She was dark and beautiful (he always preferred dark women, except Gladys Cooper, Elizabeth Bergner, and me). But Mary was not much of an actress. The two Tearles now played together all the time, but managements were not over-enthusiastic about her and she grew jealous of her husband's talent. I suppose she was hurt. They had been on the same level, but then he began to rise and she did not. It sounded very like Zelda and Scott Fitzgerald. Married to a marvellous writer, Zelda wanted to write too. Actually she did write a novel, *Save Me the Waltz*, which I thought brilliant. Godfrey did not talk to me much about his first marriage. But he once said "I must have been very dull to be married to." They were not happy, and after a time she began to drink too much.

He finally arrived in London when still in his early twenties. After many small parts, which he agreed with me were fiendishly difficult, he was offered a part by Beerbohm Tree. The son accepted what his father had refused – to work for Tree. Godfrey was given a role in an elaborate and hugely popular version of *Faust*. During the rehearsals, when he and Tree had a dramatic sword fight, every time Tree's sword touched the blade of Godfrey's there were great flying sparks. Godfrey groaned loudly, and clutched at his sword arm. He was getting agonising electric shocks. Tree looked sympathetic, and remarked that it was odd, sparks also came out of his sword, but he felt nothing.

"Is it," said Tree mildly, "because I am wearing an insulated glove?"

Godfrey stayed with Tree at His Majesty's for some time, playing many different parts but he told me that he was never happy there and that Tree treated him very badly. It is curious, for the picture one gets of Tree in his biographies is one of an urbane kindly man. Perhaps he had been deeply offended, outraged, when all those years ago Osmond Tearle had refused the honour of playing with him. For whatever reason, Godfrey never forgot how he had disliked working for Tree. He was given a dressing-room at the top of the building, a positive attic, and he had what he thought was painful indigestion. It was so bad that there were times when he rolled on the floor.

Audiences had begun to look out for Godfrey Tearle and to admire his handsome looks and stage presence. He left Tree with relief, after the most unhappy period of his career, and worked for another great actor-manager, George Alexander. Then just before the Great War, Godfrey appeared in a play by Somerset Maugham, *The Land of Promise*. It was a modern version of *The Taming of the Shrew*, and in that famous battle of the sexes Godfrey became a star. He had been acting since he was eight and a half. Yet in a way success came easily.

After that he appeared in two Barrie plays at the same time. He was Captain Hook in the afternoons, and the romantic lead in *Quality Street* in the evenings. Theatre people always enjoy nicknames, and the company called Godfrey Captain Tearle of Barrie's Own. The young Noel Coward was in the cast of *Peter Pan*, playing one of the Lost Boys.

"He was thirteen," Godfrey said. "An extraordinary child. I used to see him sitting on the deck of the pirate ship during rehearsals, muttering to himself 'I'll show 'em. I'll show 'em.'"

When Godfrey, like every other young man in England, went into the army, it was pretty difficult for Mary. She was still playing sometimes – although by now she did not play with her husband – but Godfrey's success meant that she had become used to being wealthy. Suddenly they became quite poor, for most actors never save and Godfrey had spent every penny. With a touching somersault of character, Mary behaved very well when things were difficult. She moved to Aldershot, lived in shabby digs like every other army wife. She ironed Godfrey's shirts and looked after him devotedly.

Godfrey did not tell me much about the war except to remark,

"The first person I saw when I went to the Front was Ernest Thesiger. He was wearing a string of pearls and cleaning out the latrines."

It was when the war ended that Godfrey, returning to the theatre, appeared in the spectacular melodrama which became a legend. People still mention it sometimes and smile. It was at Drury Lane, and was the stage version of a hugely popular book by Robert Hichens, *The Garden of Allah*.

The story tells of a monk who falls passionately in love and breaks his vows of poverty, chastity and obedience. He marries the women he loves, but his conscience and faith will not let him be happy. He gives her up and returns to the monastery. Godfrey was ideal casting for the hero. He had purity and masculinity and physical passion. He had a good deal of poetic suffering to do, and a ten minute long soliloquy.

As for the production, it had everything a theatregoer's heart could desire. There was a baby camel, a desert caravan, dancing dervishes in howling winds, and – the pièce de resistance – a real sandstorm. On the first night the storm swept over the actors and advanced to the first twelve rows of the stalls. It covered the elegant audience in evening dress from head to foot in sand. The reason for this disaster was that the gauze curtain designed to protect the audience from the storm's ravages did not come down in time. Audiences are always good sports, and even the sandy ones roared their applause, springing to their feet to shout "Tearle! Tearle!"

To be a star in the 1920s was very social, and Godfrey and Mary lived the life of what was then called high society. Mary took to it. The poor days at Aldershot were behind her and she lived in the richest possible way. In his big press-cutting books which I used to read on the floor because they were too heavy to keep on my lap, there were scores of pictures of Mary in the *Tatler* and the *Sketch*. She was swathed in sables, or wore elaborate dresses with fringes of gold beads and trains and evening wraps with collars and cuffs of fox at opening nights. She was more a woman of society than an actress now, although she did still play opposite Godfrey sometimes. I have two programmes of plays in which Mary Malone appeared with Godfrey. In one, *The Acquittal*, she is billed in quite large letters below him. Godfrey directed the play and it was preceded by "Godfrey Tearle in selections from his Shakespearean and other Repertoire."

Godfrey enjoyed his success and his rich life. Chow dogs, golden brown with black tongues, were fashionable, so the Tearles had two highly-bred chows which Godfrey walked round the park every day; they needed a lot of exercise. In the evenings after a performance he went to Ciro's, the Embassy or the Four Hundred where he danced with splendid women. At the theatre the queues every day waited for hours for the chance of seeing his tall broad-shouldered figure and of managing to get a scrawled signature on their programmes. Girls wrote begging him to marry them. That was the time when the diamonds and pearls hurtled on to the stage at his feet.

"It must have been fun," I said, listening.

"It was."

Actors were more light-hearted about work then. They could play in a long-running success (*The Garden of Allah* ran for a year), and then off they would go to a party or to dance until the small hours. Godfrey acted and lived with zest. I suppose he had come to accept that his marriage wasn't good, but there was so much to replace that. Or so he thought.

Then when he was still at the height of his pop-star

fame, he met a girl called Stella Freeman. She was in a play with him, playing what Godfrey called "a tennis part". He fell helplessly in love with her. Stella was in her twenties, half Godfrey's age, an uncomplicated girl whom he described to me as the heart of his life. He made up his mind very quickly that he wanted to marry her.

So after more than twenty years, there had to be a divorce. Mary had left London by that time, settling in the South of France in the luxury which Godfrey's large salaries provided. She liked still being the wife of a famous man, although she now had a lover in France. Godfrey had to bribe her to agree to the divorce; it cost him a great deal of money and some hard feelings. He was President of Equity then, and due for a knighthood. But the divorce stopped it. To be divorced in those days put you beyond the pale, as well as keeping you out of the Royal Enclosure at Ascot. Godfrey wasn't worried about that. He never wanted to be a leader in his profession. He liked acting very much, but often said to me,

"Jill, if I'd been a plumber, I'd have been a good one."

Getting his divorce was conducted in an old-fashioned positively gallant way. Godfrey and Stella went to a hotel and sat up all night playing cards. Her mother was staying at the hotel too, and called in to join a game or two.

Stella and Godfrey married, and were happy. She had a happy nature. She was not a particularly good actress, had never been ambitious, and would have cheerfully given up her career and devoted her life to him. She was a bonny, fresh-faced girl with a mass of curling brown hair and an open-air candid sort of beauty. She had no attacks of Celtic glooms; she was even-tempered and merry. The two girls who came into Godfrey's life were very different . . . and I never would have been in his life at all had Stella lived. She already had a delicate chest when he first met her. When they married, he built her a house in the country near Tring – he called the house "Busker's End". The air in the Chiltern Hills was supposed to be good for the lungs. But after four happy years, Godfrey's young wife died.

I was not jealous of the idea of Stella, although I knew how deeply he had loved her. Her pretty face stared out of a frame in his bedroom. She looked carefree. And I know if I had asked "Was Stella prettier than me?" the answer would have been, "She was."

Then we would go on talking about *my* deep love, the theatre, and the successes and failures of the past. Sometimes I read Godfrey's old notices. Mostly, they praised almost too much, they seemed to be all raves. But there was a phrase, describing his performance in 1921 as a successful soldier in *The Faithful Heart* which I thought – I still think – exactly described his acting. "Manly feeling and an almost womanly sympathy."

I liked hearing about the romantic parts that Godfrey used to play: a Mountie in the Canadian Mounted Police, flashing his eyes at the heroine who refused him and crying "By God. You shall!" Godfrey played in rubbish, with titles like *A Good Girl's Crossroads* and *The Ugliest Woman in the World*. There was a piece which a critic described as "contemporary mush" called *Dancing Mothers* about the Bright Young Things, and the following year he was in a musical called *Merely Molly*. Then he would play Mirabell in *The Way of the World*, and then in 1931 he appeared as *Hamlet*. Godfrey did not agonise over whether a part suited him or not. As he had said of his parents – he just went out and did it.

Those were the days of enormous charity shows blazing with stars. They raised thousands of pounds, and the programmes were printed on real silk. Godfrey was always asked to appear; he was one of the big names to pull in the wealthy customers. He played in musicals and melodramas, his life was a kaleidoscope of roles of every kind. He played in uniform or blacked up in *Aloma of the South Seas*. He suffered in a monk's cassock, or spoke epigrams when wearing impeccable tails. He acted in wheelchairs, in velvets, in nonsense and in Shakespeare. He played opposite Tallulah Bankhead when she was cast as a girl pure as the driven snow. Godfrey said that his part was yet another By God You Shall! In their love scene, Tallulah was supposed to give him a little chaste embrace. Instead she kissed him so violently that he could not break away to say his next line, her lips remained glued to his.

He told me something about his old trick of being able to roll a cigarette with one hand. Walter Hackett, the playwright, saw him doing that, and used it at the end of one of his plays. Godfrey was the detective in disguise, and at the final confrontation, the detective's identity had to be proved.

"He could – roll a cigarette with one hand," said somebody to Godfrey. "*Can you?*"

Godfrey did.

Godfrey quoted me one of his bad notices. It was when he took over Hamlet from Henry Ainley.

"Godfrey Tearle played the part as if he had just taken his double blue at Wittenberg."

J. C. Trewin recalls Godfrey in the 1930s. He saw him as Henry V, as Mark Antony in *Julius Caesar* at the Alhambra in Leicester Square in 1934, before the huge old theatre was demolished. It was, he said,

the last of the old Shakespeare seasons. It was received rather roughly then. New ways of acting and directing Shakespeare had begun to be seen. But I remember how excited I was by Godfrey

159

Tearle's ease. He was in supreme command, almost a lazy command. He spoke Shakespeare with understanding and appreciation and almost with relish. Most of the speaking then, except for the Gielgud school, was pretty bad. It was sheer joy to sit back and listen and look. I was Godfrey Tearle's man from then on.

But he considered that during most of the 1930s Godfrey had been thrown away. He was "several times larger than life in very small modern plays".

Godfrey did get away from those when he worked again with his old friend James Barrie, who had written *The Boy David* especially for Elizabeth Bergner. Godfrey played King Saul. The play was directed by Komisarjevsky and designed by Augustus John. Godfrey thought Elizabeth Bergner was magical.

"You're a bit like her," he said to me once. Then he paused and added,

"Only a bit."

His compliments always ended in a put-down.

Like the good actor that he was, he would stop his stories while I still longed for more. No, he said, he wouldn't continue. I must wait until the next day.

While I think about Godfrey talking to me, I can hear his voice again. It was extraordinary. I wish I could make it echo in the printed word, I wish I had the skill. The critics who wrote about it used phrases which now seem over the top. They call his voice "silver tongued" or say that it had "noble arpeggios". They say it is "delightful", "magnificent", even "pure and sweet". None of those seems right. In his old recordings, too, there is something missing, some tone of his voice has escaped.

They say that men are seduced by what they see, women by what they hear. I used to sit on the floor and listen to Godfrey's voice. When I remember us then, it seems to me that we were not unlike Othello and Desdemona when they first met, and he began to tell her the story of his life.

> She lov'd me for the dangers I had pass'd;
> And I lov'd her that she did pity them.
> This only is the witchcraft I have us'd.

Seven

It was foggy that winter. Those were not the fogs we grumble about now, which are dangerous to traffic and maddening to travellers but still clean, if impenetrable, white mists. The fogs pressing against the windows of Queen Anne Street, which muffled the sound of cars and took silent possession of the city, were pea-soupers. They had not altered much since the days of Dickens: they were greenish, stifling, filthy and tasting of sulphur. There were flares in the streets giving a limited uncanny light, and you could literally get lost walking home down a street you had known all your life.

Godfrey was at the New Theatre in *The Hanging Judge*. The play, from the novel by Bruce Marshall, had been adapted by Raymond Massey, an old friend from Hollywood days, and directed by another old friend, the formidable Michael Powell. He rarely directed plays but had decided to do this one because Godfrey was to play the lead, a pitiless and much-hated judge who is caught and eventually sentenced for a crime he never committed. The play had dramatic, even melodramatic scenes, including one where the judge suffered a complete moral collapse.

The Hanging Judge was having a reasonable success (some critics did not like it), but Godfrey's health worried me more and more. The fogs troubled him. The effect was frightening, for his breathing was not good. During the fogs it was impossible for him to be collected by car. He had to travel home late at night after the show on the Underground, and walk from Oxford Circus through that horrible air.

162

Godfrey had been ill twice already. Once he'd been told by the doctors that he must stay in bed. He remained at home in Queen Anne Street, and behaved very badly.

On the second occasion, he went into a nursing home for a short spell.

He had become very thin.

"You should have something decent to eat between the matinee and evening performances," I said.

He did not look particularly interested.

"I'll bring you something," I said. "I shall go to Sheekey's."

Sheekey's is still there in St. Martin's Court which runs down the side of what was then the New and is now the Albery Theatre. It is a lively pleasant restaurant, and Godfrey and I lunched there quite often. They specialise in fish, which he liked best. So on the raw dark Wednesdays and Saturdays, at six in the evening, I would be at Sheekey's collecting little hot casseroles of halibut meunière. I took them up to Godfrey's dressing-room, made a space on the table, and sat down to watch him eat.

How did he feel? I asked.

He ignored that.

"You're being very attentive," he said ironically, "Tell me about the radio work. What happened to-day?"

I was not in a play then, but I had been given a lot of radio work and he was really pleased about that. Unlike all those maids, opening the play by sweeping the floor, unlike the giggling ladies-in-waiting, I was given leading parts on the radio. If you start with big parts the magic goes on and you continue to be offered them. Even my very first role, when I had left Cornwall to go to the B.B.C. in Birmingham, had been quite large. There was never a serving maid in sight. Now I was playing leads and working with important actors like Esmé Percy, Edith Evans, Howard Marion Craw-ford, and for directors famous in broadcasting, Archie Campbell, Frederick Bradenham and Donald McWhinnie.

I have always loved radio. You have to think clearly and strongly, but there are no parts you cannot play because you are physically unsuitable. You can play a radiant beauty or a girl with a hare lip like the heroine of *Precious Bane*; you can play a French princess or a fat trollop. Radio consists only of the voice and the im-agination of actor and audience. It is pure. And there's another thing about radio; actors will always be glad to work for six or seven days to do radio work, whereas you could never manage to collect a star-packed cast for a run. When I played Goneril in *King Lear* on the radio, for instance, there was Alec Guinness, Cyril Cusack, Sarah Badel, Norman Rodway, Eileen Atkins, Ronald Pickup and Robert Powell. Brilliant actors, some of whom only arrived to play in one episode.

Radio was the work that Godfrey approved for me most, and he liked to hear everything about it. He taught me the pleasure of describing the details of the day, the food, the clothes, the moments of fun, the flip conversations, the smells, the colours. No detail bored him, he could not have enough, and often murmured encouragingly, "Yes. Go on."

When he was not playing at the theatre, or being with me, he still saw his friends, including Margaret Leighton. He loved actresses, particularly leading actresses. He was, for instance, totally dedicated to Katharine Hepburn. When she came to England to play in Shaw's *The Millionairess* in 1952, he saw her performance seventeen times. He only took me once. I was never asked when he took Margaret Leighton out to the Savoy. Although she was very nice to me, I did have a pang or two. As he had said, she was a real actress. I hadn't got there yet.

When the fog cleared and London was itself again, there was my birthday – and Christmas to celebrate. My birthday is on Christmas Eve which is one of the worst days of the year to have been born. But Godfrey, like my mother, always gave me two presents. This year, 1952, we celebrated by going to the Old Vic to see *Romeo and Juliet*, in which Alan Badel was a brilliant Romeo. After the play Godfrey took me, and Peter Finch who had played Mercutio, out to supper. It was typical of Godfrey's unselfishness that he spent the whole evening talking enthusiastically about Peter Finch's performance. He and Finch had become really good friends by then.

We would eat at the Caprice, or rather just as in the old days at the Cobweb, I ate and Godfrey didn't. People came over to greet him. I remember Noel Coward coming to our table, and Godfrey's exclamation, "Hello, my angel! You look ravishing!" He had an absurd, a positively flirtatious, manner with men, he was outrageous, kissing them on the cheek as if he were a French general and holding their hands. I don't know how it was, but he was never camp. He just looked affectionate and funny.

We rarely went to parties, Godfrey and I. He did not like them and preferred to dine with a few friends. I think I *did* like them, but parties were more glamorous then, perhaps because of the clothes. We liked dolling ourselves up to the nines, but now unless it is for Glyndebourne or Henley we never do. Godfrey wore a big actorish camel-hair coat which was most dramatic. He looked like Diaghilev. He took me to Burberry's and bought me one as well. "You're not up to a mink," he said. In return, because I never could find a present he wanted, I bought him a bunch of cornflowers. He liked those. Cornflowers became his favourite flowers and whenever I could get them, he wore one in his buttonhole.

He liked late nights, going out to supper after the show, he never had been a man for poached eggs and a glass of weak whisky and water after seeing a play. We went to the Café de Paris to see Marlene Dietrich, and later we went to see Noel Coward. We met him afterwards. He was very spirited and made wonderful jokes, but I thought him rather frightening. I did a lot of things in London with Godfrey that I had never done before, and it was not necessary to be cool about them. It was not necessary, either, to pretend. If things were exciting it did not matter if I showed it. Godfrey preferred that.

I was working at my radio, and in between broadcasts I suffered from the usual certainty that my career (yet again) was over. Godfrey was busy that winter as he always was, seeing directors and film people, trying to set things up. Many of them, like houses of cards, suddenly collapsed. And all the time, over and over again, he would try to arrange for another production of *Macbeth*.

Stratford had been the only time we played together, and one of the plays Godfrey was interested in reviving was Emlyn Williams's *The Light of Heart*, for me to play the girl and Godfrey his role of the ageing actor. But I was too inexperienced and the idea made me nervous. I did not feel up to working with Godfrey. I needed practice.

The New Year was beginning, 1953, heralded as Coronation year and already the newspapers were full of news about royalty. I scarcely noticed. Godfrey was not well, although he was so busy. We both knew it. When *The Hanging Judge* closed, his doctor said that he should have a holiday, and Godfrey agreed. The sun, said the doctor, would do him good. Godfrey did not want a holiday much; he agreed to go as if it were a duty to himself. We both decided that Madeira was far enough away for there to be sunshine.

To fly to Madeira then you had to take a flying boat. We set off cheerfully enough, although he looked tired and pale. But during the flight (the cabins then were not pressurised) he had a heart attack and became dreadfully ill. For a terrified few minutes I thought he was going to die. He recovered, and somehow or other when the journey was over we got ourselves to Reid's hotel. I saw with trembling relief that he had some colour again.

"We ought to get a doctor," I said.

"I suppose so."

We saw not one doctor, but two. They examined him and were concerned and both gave us different suggestions. One said he must not drink – the other recommended Scotch. A third doctor, this time a Portuguese, spoke to me when I saw him out. He said very gently, "Senorita. Your friend is dying."

I said I knew. And thanked him for coming. The truth was that I *did* know Godfrey was fatally ill, I had known for months about his weak heart but refused to think about it. Like Scarlett O'Hara, I shoved the knowledge to the back of my mind. I would think about it tomorrow.

Godfrey did not enjoy the holiday in Madeira, in fact he hated it. We were staying at the famous Reid's hotel in Funchal. It stands in gardens leading in terraces to the sea and was quite as splendid in those days as any hotel in Godfrey's rich past. Funchal was small, with old whitewashed houses, some with courtyards and fountains. The streets were lined with jacaranda trees, and behind the hotel the hillsides were terraced like a great staircase. From my room, I could hear the noise of the sea. In the soft warm weather, flowers began to come out. It was like a late and lovely English spring.

But Godfrey wasn't well enough to do a thing. He couldn't sail in the bright sea, he couldn't even swim.

He came down to the pool or the beach and watched me. He couldn't play tennis, but watched me doing that, with some young acquaintances from the hotel. Godfrey had always been a very physical person who enjoyed swimming, ski-ing, tennis, dancing, golf. It must have been misery to watch someone doing all the things he used to enjoy and do so well.

I know now how he must have felt, because I have never outgrown my love of the ballet. At school I studied it, and later I had the chance of a scholarship to the Royal Ballet, but I chose words instead of movement and the short life of the dancer. Yet I love dancing still and when I watch dancers taking class I long and long to jump up and join them.

When it was known on the island that Godfrey Tearle was staying at Reid's, invitations came asking him to dine. He was feted and made much of. We went to the imposing house of the Blandys (he was the shipping tycoon) who had lived for some time in Madeira. We met all kinds of people who knew Godfrey, from actors to sportsmen. We changed into our formal clothes for dinner. We sat and sunbathed. But Godfrey's health was in both our thoughts. Before we had left London the doctor said Godfrey must have injections and asked me if I could manage to give them. I said cheerfully, "Of course."

"It'll be useful when I get a part in one of his films like *White Corridors*," I said.

I had to give the injections. I became quite skilful, but he was so thin that it was difficult to find a spot on his thigh in which to put the needle, and we made jokes about that.

I went on refusing to allow myself to think; I concentrated on amusing him. We talked. Did it tire him? Did I talk too much? I don't know. We often talked until after midnight and he would always say, "Oh, don't go yet."

We had been in Madeira for about a week when I received a telegram from London. Godfrey was on the terrace, and I stood at the reception desk and opened the telegram without much enthusiasm. I was pre-occupied.

"Imperative you return London at once. Audition for Alan Ladd film *Hell Below Zero*," said the wire. It was from my agent.

I stood in the foyer and looked at it. My big chance at last? I made a grimace and shoved the telegram in my pocket. I had no intention of returning to London at once. It didn't seem important. I was not going to leave Godfrey or tell him about the telegram. I wired saying it was impossible to go back.

The good weather broke, it began to rain heavily. We stayed indoors playing Canasta. We had drinks with some people he knew. They were in the music business and very lively, talking about a world I knew nothing about, the tough wheeling and dealing in Charing Cross Road.

Godfrey and I, alone later on that day, sat looking out of the hotel windows at the rain and the sea.

"You'll be glad when it's time to go home," I said. "Won't you?"

But we stayed the full fortnight we had arranged. Once or twice during that time there were people at the hotel who looked at us with the unmistakable expression I had often seen in London; and was going to meet more often in the months to come. It was a look of disapproval mixed with dislike. And fear. I don't know why. Because they didn't understand about Godfrey and me, and people always seem to be afraid of things they don't understand.

At last the day came for our return flight. Godfrey seemed better and, although I was tense during the flight, he was not worried by it. When the train finally drew in at Waterloo, he picked up our suitcases and literally ran down the platform. He turned to me and laughed.

"I suddenly feel better. Thank God we're back!"

When we met a friend of his that evening who asked "How was the holiday?" Godfrey promptly said "Horrible!"

We had not been home for twenty-four hours in Queen Anne Street when my agent rang. I was expecting reproaches and answered curtly, but all he said was that they had not yet cast the part in the Alan Ladd film and still wanted to see me.

Godfrey was delighted when he heard the news. He didn't know I had already been asked for while we had been away. He positively beamed before I left for the studios. He said I must not be nervous.

"Just go out and show your quality and your fighting spirit."

I didn't feel I had either when I arrived at the studios, but I swept in looking as if I had. To my surprise, it seemed that I was not being given an audition at all. I discovered later that John Huston had talked to Mark Robson, the director of the film, and said, "Don't test her. If you do, you won't give her the part. Don't test her and she'll get it."

Instead of a test, I was asked to do a reading. Anthony Bushell the actor, who was also one of the directors of Laurence Olivier productions, was associate producer on the film; he read the Alan Ladd part opposite me.

Hell Below Zero was set in a whaling station in Norway and the part I read for was that of a physically strong tomboyish girl, daughter of the captain of the station. When her father has to go away, she is temporarily left in charge. It can't have been my questionable Scandinavian accent which pleased them. Perhaps it was the way I looked. They gave me the part. Work. Riches. Even fame?

I rushed home to the flat where I found Godfrey in the sitting room, the inevitable script on his lap. He looked up.

"You got it."

"Godfrey! Twenty-five pounds a day for twenty-one days!"

"Excellent. You can buy me another boat knife."

I had never seen him so pleased, never for anything of his own. After my first day of filming he wanted me to tell him every detail, and later during the shooting he came down to the studios and met Alan Ladd.

Every morning when I arrived at the studios, I was dressed in costume – whaling clothes. There were great heavy boots, oiled sweaters (memories of Cornwall), and a red knitted hat. My hair had to be very short, so I cut it myself with my nail scissors to look like a boy's, leaving the ends jagged. The make-up people greased my face until it shone.

My first lines, in my not-so-Swedish accent, were to Alan Ladd.

"How do you do, Mr. Craig. My name is Gerda Petersen. And you will be my first mate."

Looking at myself in the glaringly-lit mirrors of the make-up department, I saw a girl who was not exactly the best-dressed woman in the world. Cropped and jagged hair, greasy face. But I was enjoying myself more than I've ever done except on the radio. I had a real part.

Alan Ladd was kind, good looking and, above everything, he was cool. Like a Scott Fitzgerald hero, he always wore white. I never saw him without his toupee of fair silky hair and his ears almost invisibly taped back. He had beautiful green eyes which were infinitely expressive. He could have been a wonderful actor, but he cut almost every line he had to speak. He merely said things like "Let's go," or "I kinda like you."

Everybody knows that Alan Ladd was very short and that to make him look taller, he always stood on a box when he was in shot. The shots never went below the knee. Once during a shooting Mark Robson said to me, "Get closer to Alan." I made the mistake of climbing up on the box with him. I was ordered down at once.

Most of the best scenes in the film, the really exciting ones, were done by the stunt-men. But to me everything was wonderful, and Alan was extraordinarily helpful to me, a girl so new at film-making. He was a strange man. He always walked around accompanied by his stand-in who looked uncannily like him and who also always wore white. At a distance they looked exactly like identical twins. Alan had an entourage, as one imagines a gangster might have – or a Hollywood star, I suppose. People hung about all the time at his beck and call. John Goodwin told me that when he was working at Stratford Chico Marx came to the theatre, and he, too, had six or seven people who went with him everywhere. When Chico said he'd like to look round backstage, the whole group went too.

Driving to the studios early one morning in Godfrey's car, the Dolomite, the brakes went and I crashed. Only into the side of the road, mercifully, but there I was, stranded. Alan Ladd's Rolls came round the corner while I was standing helplessly by my car. He was in the back in his white suit. He signalled the chauffeur to stop and wound down the window.

"Well," he said. "That's life, kid."

And drove away.

Godfrey enjoyed my stories. When I came home in the evening after filming, I had something to talk about again, something to amuse and interest him. I told him about Alan Ladd and about my lessons for my Scandinavian accent. I told him about the cast, the director, everything. We talked late into the night,

perhaps too late, but he still always said "Don't go." In
exchange, he told me a few stories too. Once he said,
"Did I tell you about a play I did called *The Faithful
Heart*? There was a sentence in it which shocked
London. It was when my daughter said to me – 'But
Father, you are illegitimate.'"

Godfrey was not working, except for doing a com-
mentary of some kind for an Alec Guinness film.
Robert Hardy came to see him one evening while I was
still at the studios, and scolded him.

"Godfrey, you're very lazy, sitting about like that.
You know what you should be doing? Preparing to
play Lear."

"But I didn't know," Robert said to me later, "that
Godfrey was preparing to die."

While I was still filming *Hell Below Zero* Godfrey
became ill again. At first he was irritated when the
doctor said he should go into hospital. But then suddenly he wasn't difficult about it. That scared me more
than anything.

Very well, he said, he would go into a nursing
home. But why couldn't I come and stay too?

I packed both our suitcases and we moved in
together to the Bentinck Street Nursing Home. The
matron, with no comment, gave me a small room not
far from his.

I was at the studios every day and living in a nursing
home at night. London was festive, preparing for the
Coronation. I didn't seem to take that in, and when I
look back at those weeks, I do not remember anything
about it.

I spent every moment that I could in Godfrey's
room. I went on telling him my saga of every day of the
filming, and I ate enormous meals. It seemed absolutely necessary to eat when I was with him, to show
that I felt optimistic. Plates and plates of tomato sandwiches came into the room, ordered by Godfrey be-

cause he knew they were my favourite. His own food
was sent in every day by Mario at the Caprice. That
was not Godfrey's idea, it was Mario's because he was
fond of him.

Sometimes I was asked to go downstairs to see the
doctors. I had meetings with them in a private waiting
room. They must have thought it curious to talk to a
young girl, an actress, and consult her as if she were an
experienced and wise adult. Sir Horace Evans, the
heart specialist who had looked after George V and
Queen Mary too, talked to me. I didn't know how to
handle all that, except to be very polite and attentive
and leave the decisions to them.

Sir Horace told me that Godfrey had a tired heart.
Nowadays with pacemakers and heart surgery he
could have been saved. But Sir Horace, like the kind
Portuguese doctor in Madeira, knew that Godfrey was
dying.

While I was at the studios during the day, Godfrey
had far far too many visitors. Margaret Leighton came
often, and his old love Gladys Cooper, and Binkie
Beaumont, the head of H. M. Tennent's, and his agent
Olive Harding who was so fond of him. Being Godfrey, he turned his stay at Bentinck Street into a social
whirl. Was it unwise? Why should it be? What was he
saving himself *for*, I thought, and knew he thought the
same.

He still had a little hope left, and once when I came
back from filming he was cheerful and optimistic. He
said he had had a dream. He had been lying surrounded by something black, all this black stuff which
had been the illness and which had come out of his
body and left him. He spoke again and again about the
dream which made him feel so cheerful. I ate another
sandwich, and he asked me practical questions. Had I
remembered to insure the aquamarine ring? Had he
remembered to tell me that he had left most of his

money to charity? I said, yes, the ring was insured, and none of that talk about wills, please, it was jolly boring. He winked.

I wasn't filming on the day he died, and I was with him all day, holding his hand. I was really tired from getting up at the crack of dawn, driving to the studios, filming and rushing back to Bentinck Street. I got into bed with Godfrey, as I often did, and lay beside him. I just lay and held his hand.

He died in the middle of the night. Just before he died he said rather firmly, in an active kind of voice,

"You are my sunshine."

I rang the bell and a nurse came in.

He was dead.

I climbed out of bed. The nurse went to fetch the matron, who came into the room, looked at Godfrey for a moment, and then turned to me.

"Will you please go. Leave my hospital," she said.

I was slightly dazed, and then I saw that look which I had seen in many faces, and which had been concealed all the time Godfrey had been ill. I said fiercely.

"With the greatest of pleasure," and walked out.

I changed into my day clothes and went into the street. It was two in the morning.

The next day my mother took me back to the nursing home, and when the matron saw her she was all polite smiles and courtesy. My mother was very cold. We were taken up to that familiar room, my mother came with me, and then she left me alone.

I looked at Godfrey who was lying so still. He looked handsome, noble and quite unfamiliar. Was it really him? He had one little toe which grew slightly overlapping the next. Going over to the bed, I lifted the sheet to make absolutely sure that it *was* him. And it was.

I remember as I walked home with my mother in

silence that I thought – it's funny, someone like Godfrey dying. I felt somehow that he was going to be
immortal.

It was some days later that I went back, like a
homing pigeon, to Godfrey's flat. Not long before he
died, he had said to me,

"I can't hang on very much longer. Are you going to
be all right?"

"Absolutely fine."

"Do you want to live in the flat? You can."

"Oh, that's not important. I'll think about it. Let me
tell you what happened at the studios today . . ."

So now I walked towards the building which had
been my home and walked up the steps and rang the
bell. I'd forgotten my key.

The man who looked after Godfrey, the ex-major
who had always disliked me, opened the door. I had
literally forgotten about him and how he felt and when
he saw me his face went purple. He lifted up his stick
and hit me.

I was too numb to feel the blow. I think it was from
jealousy; and because he thought I had killed Godfrey
with my love.

I didn't cry at all after Godfrey died. I felt relieved.
When he was very ill I had thought over and over
again – Oh, I wish he'd hurry up and go, I wish he'd
go. He had been brave but he so hated it, he was so fed
up. That sounds a stupid thing to say but it was exactly
how he felt. He was so self-reliant, he detested having
things done for him. Some people can bear illness
heroically, but he wasn't like that. He was worn out
after being his stylish, worldly, charitable, lovely,
unruffled self during four years of fading health. His
strength had been used up and there was nothing left.

When somebody dies it is dramatic, and however

much you think you are ready for it, you never are. I was busy and I hadn't time to think. Godfrey had left me all his possessions. I went to the flat a second time, taking his agent and friend Olive Harding. I believe my mother arranged for the ex-major not to be there. We went through all Godfrey's things and I gave most of them away. I kept a few books of press cuttings, an ash tray with a penny set in it, which had been his contract with Charles Morgan for *The Flashing Stream*. His blue tobacco jar. And a prompt copy of *Macbeth*, and one of *Othello* in the margin of which, scrawled in Godfrey's writing, was "Get through this speech as quickly as possible. It is *very* boring."

He left me a letter. I won't quote it, I can't bear to. It was a very positive letter and filled with encouragement. He was afraid that I would never manage without him, and he wrote "You *must* find happiness." Because he knew that, if I did not, our four years together would all have been a mistake.

One odd thing happened during those dazed days. A number of people turned up and claimed that they were Godfrey's illegitimate children. Who were they and what became of them? The lawyer coped with them, I suppose. He told me later that this often happens when a famous person dies.

Godfrey had once told me, when we were in Cornwall I think, that after his death he would like his ashes to be scattered on the sea. I don't think I remembered that after he died. Or if I did, then somebody wrongly told me it was no longer allowed. That isn't true. There are no laws against that last sea-loving gesture. I wish I had remembered. I wish I had known. He left a note in his will to say he did not want flowers at his funeral. That any of his friends who wanted to remember him would perhaps be kind enough to send the money to charity. But I went out and bought a seven and six-penny bunch of cornflowers. Sometimes you must do the opposite of what has been asked of you, for your own sake. The cornflowers were the only way I had left to show my love.

Years after Godrey died, when I first met John Osborne, I had to go off to Turkey for the filming of *The Charge of the Light Brigade*. When I returned, he told me he had written a play, and thought that I would be pleased with it. It was *Time Present*.

I suppose as a writer John Osborne found the two characters, Godfrey and myself, interesting. I had talked to him a great deal about Godfrey – he was one of the few people I did tell about him. He understood him. *Time Present* was not only written about Godfrey, it was *to* him in a way.

The Godfrey character is called Orme, and when the play opens he is already dying. He never actually appears, and he is the best character in the play. I was his daughter, a very obsessive daughter who loved him. Daughter and father were terribly close. The title, *Time Present*, refers to the fact that when her father dies, she knows she will be rudderless. She doesn't know what she is going to do with her life.

It is very, very well written and observed, and I say "observed" because, although John Osborne never met Godfrey, he got him absolutely right. I adored being in *Time Present*. I enjoyed speaking about Godfrey onstage, and thinking about him too. There was such a lot of him in the play.

We opened at the Royal Court, then *Hotel in Amsterdam*, also by John Osborne, came in. One critic picked up the fact that Orme was based on Godfrey, calling him stupidly in his notice, a "boulevard actor". Anthony Page who had directed the play made short work of that critic. Anyway, what is a boulevard actor? Somebody who played everything from Shakespeare to melodrama, who began his career in the theatre at eight and a half, who became one of the great figures and was adored all his life?

A great many people were very kind to me in the weeks after Godfrey's death. Kenneth Tynan, who had deeply admired him, told me he wanted to write a marvellous obituary. Did he? I don't know, because I read and remembered nothing. His friends wanted to give a memorial service but Godfrey had said he did not want that, so I stopped it. That came into *Time Present*.

"Orme," says the daughter, "would have hated the idea. I don't think he ever went to a memorial service in his life. He'd have laughed his head off at the idea, rows of his friends having to listen to Handel and Wesley and knighted actors reading the lesson. He'd have thought it very common."

That was exactly what Godfrey would have thought.

The first six months after Godfrey died were all right for me. But the next two years were hard, sometimes too hard. I had lost my bearings. But I was always losing those . . .

Writing about Godfrey has given me pain but a lot of pleasure too. Seeing him at a distance yet still vividly, has made me feel optimistic. Most of the good things I know are because of him. He taught me about loving friendship between men and women, he taught me about acting, and how to keep a sense of humour and never to be ashamed of being emotional. And what's so bad, he said, about having a bad temper? Sometimes he would say "Have a good cry. And have a good laugh."

I suppose he did teach me to expect too much. I thought other people were going to be like that, and of course they were not. I felt related to him, not as if he were my father – I had a fine father – but as if he had filled the space in my life which had always been there because I was an only child. I'm ashamed to think how when I was with him I so often fretted about my career. But he had such a calming effect on me, because he believed in me, I suppose. Just sitting with him gave me confidence. He never took me over, although we were so much together. He was the freest spirit I have ever met, and free in the way he treated me.

Celibacy, and big love affairs, suit me. They suited him. Just as friendship suited us both so well. I knew I was plain. He used to say, with his energy, "You are immensely attractive." I was a tomboy. But I was a woman too, or I never would have been with him.

There are things I still find difficult. Going to Cornwall, for instance. Watching Godfrey on screen is an active masochism, and listening to him on the few tapes which I have is painful/enjoyable. I love to talk about him to the few people who remember him, and I know that if I caught sight of an original Triumph Dolomite my heart would turn over.

Sometimes when I'm walking in London, I see a car or a taxi with the number KGT. I always think that's going to bring me luck. Somebody gave Godfrey a number plate with those letters, after he was knighted. They were meant to stand for Knight, Godfrey Tearle. He thought that quite awful, but was too lazy to change it.

I have loved since Godfrey died, but never been so well pleased, so all-enveloped, so full of trust. Real love is different from being in love because you don't have to tell each other lies. It was so obvious that we were utterly unsuitable, he and I. It never was going to be a run of the mill romance.

When he left me that letter, saying that I must be happy because otherwise our four years would have been a dreadful mistake, a cruel waste, he didn't know how much he had enriched my life. Suppose, I think sometimes, I met you *now*, Godfrey. What an amazing time we'd have.

And then I think how glad I am that he walked across the room that night at Stratford, and asked if he could drive me home, and took me to the deserted airfield, wherever it was. There's something in *Great Expectations* which describes the way I feel about the first time Godfrey chose me to be with him.

That was a memorable day for me, for it made great changes in me. But, it is the same with any life. Imagine one selected day struck out of it, and think how different its course would have been. Pause, you who read this, and think for a moment of the long chain of iron or gold, of thorns or flowers, that would never have bound you, but for the formation of the first link on one memorable day.

Index

Index